Yes

Health Matters in the Workplace

How a healthy workplace culture will always provide a sense of acceptance, recognition, belonging, acknowledgment and care

Gregory Payne Bridge

Copyright © 2019

All rights reserved. This book or any portion thereof may not be reproduced or used in any manner whatsoever without the express written permission of the author except for the use of brief quotations in a book review.

Printed in Australia
First Printing, 2019
ISBN: 978-0-6484641-5-0

White Light Publishing
Melton, VIC, Australia 3337
whitelightpublishing.com.au

Acknowledgements

'Mrs Mullane, 'I have finally completed my homework.'

I would like to acknowledge her great kindness and belief in my ability when she was my English teacher in 1979, while attending Kingswood High School in New South Wales, Australia. In that year, she taught me the love of books, the value of reading and more importantly, to get something from it.

I would like to acknowledge my parents John and Christine, who instilled the worthiness of good manners and respect would pay off down the track in building future relationships. I may not have seen eye to eye with them on some views of the world at times, but they worked out it was a changing world and their son was going to be what he was going to be. My mother would have been over the moon that I had completed my homework too.

To all my close friends who have been with me and encouraged me to complete this book, and those who stood by me and graciously gave unconditional support and love for many years. I hope by reading this book I will inspire you to write your own wisdom that can be shared with the world.

Right now, people around us are looking for inspiration and encouragement to impact on the positives to the human spirit. My aim was always to do something that would come with great hope and joyfulness, as we only have one life and we don't know when that ends. We don't know what we do that will outlive us, and we should not take our workplace or community too lightly. Just remember, the possibilities are always there; to do something that lives past you, something that becomes part of our culture for the ages, and tomorrow may be the day.

Best wishes, my fellow readers. You have the choice to have a great life. Go for it and don't forget to bring others with you.

About the Author

Greg Bridge, Author, is an Aboriginal from the Gija descendants of the East Kimberley region in Western Australia. He has over 20 years of experience passionately commentating and helping with his Human Behaviour Excellence programs, on the 'authority and impact of our language use' that is slowly dehumanising our workplace. Mr Bridge is a director of GP Bridge Training and Development and the Human Behaviour Excellence Centre, based in Perth. His programs have been successful with prominent and large companies, and to several Private and State Schools, to youth enabling the participants to learn effective communications skills with positive and constructive intent.

He also holds a qualification in Musculoskeletal Therapy to aid people in their own balance and wellbeing to improve body muscular issues. Furthermore, as part of his continual passions, he commentates and researches the increasing issue of Foetal Alcohol Syndrome Disorder (FASD) which is impacting long term for both our community and individuals. In 2016 he had a year off from his business in Perth, to be a fulltime Sessional lecturer at Health Studies Unit, Notre Dame University, Broome, Western Australia. Greg was also a member of Notre Dame's, Broome, Nulungu's Research Centre Graduates Associates study group where he presented and investigated the connection of FASD and the Justice System. He is also a speaker on In Vitro Fertilisation (IVF), on 'Shifting perception on IVF', as he has an IVF son.

He is an active sports person and continues to work closely with the community in all areas and stays in touch with the grass roots of the business world.

Contents

Living with Chronic Illness in the Workplace	16
What is Chronic Illness?	32
A Business Approach to Illnesses in the Workplace	54
Shifting of the Workplace	72
Reclaiming Your Working Life	88
The Impact of Peripheral Factors	104
Behavioural Change in the Workplace	120
Where are we Headed?	136
A Call to Action: Balance your Lifestyle	152
The New Frontier of Leadership	168
The Impact of Workplace Culture	184
In Closing	200
The Human Behaviour Excellence Centre	216

Introduction

This is an opportunity to write something down and share an issue which I feel is affecting our community in many ways, and that is, chronic illness or pre-illness in the workplace, and it is now at a crisis point. It is as if we are oblivious or silent to the fact that most of the deaths in Australia and around the world are caused by illnesses and chronic illness, which in most cases are preventable, instead of losing lives and talent. More so the effects of what chronic illness is doing to our workplace environment now, in the past, and where we are heading into the future. For indeed, where are we heading for our long-term wellness in our professions? And if we do not take hold of our health issues, what is the future looking like for you and me, our families, friends, and the community?

Let me tell you a little about myself, where I am from, what my background is and what my interest is in talking and writing about chronic illness in the workplace. My family origins are my father, Joseph (John) Payne Bridge, born 1942, in Halls Creek Western Australia. His father was of European and English descent. His mother was of Aboriginal descent born in the north East of the Kimberley region of Western Australia (WA). Yes, I am of Aboriginal descent, a Gija man, my people are from the Warmun Community not far out of the town of Halls Creek in WA.

My mother, Christine Mary Bridge (birth name - Hill), was born in Singleton, N.S.W in 1943 to both parents of English heritage and European descent many generations back. I have a brother, Lindsay, my only sibling. I also have one son Jarod Bridge, and he is my only child. Now, having shown my Aboriginal and (briefly) my family heritage, and due to the highly discussed issues of Aboriginal people and their poor health which has been so well documented in Australia for the past decades or so, you may think I am writing about chronic illness and the lifestyles of Aboriginal people. Not so, this book is for everyone and it is an overview of my life's observations to the issues people face day to day 'living silently with an illness or a chronic illness in the workplace'.

There is no doubt there are many illness issues that Aboriginal people face as individuals, families, and their community at large. But chronic illness is challenging everyone and all forms of our diverse culture, and what it is doing to our workplace...but more about that later.

Let us go back to the beginning. I was a child raised in a working-class family, as they termed it in the sixties and seventies. Both of my parents, like most, were hard working, always looking towards self-growth, leading by example to develop a quality of life foremost with education, to be positive and to contribute to citizens in the community and to look at being the best providers to our family. Both of my parents drank occasionally only in social situations, but very sparingly had a glass of wine on special occasions. My father John did not like the taste of beer and both did not smoke tobacco.

I must confess as I begin this new journey of self-discovery as a writer and expressing my views, I am feeling anxious, excited and curious as to my vision of the future and where we may end up going, but hopefully I can provide some ideas to get something started and see if we can make a difference, leave a small legacy and inspire those around us to have a great life along the way, and taking better care of ourselves in our professions and the future of the workplace. My aim is to impact our community, so we can all have great lives and leave our future generations something to improve on and have fun along the way. Our health is most important to our life's journey, progress, and self-growth. Our health is also paramount to our long-term positive interaction in our professions and to building relationships in many forms, which I believe is the core existence of who we are. Noticing talented and gifted people who are unable to perform at an optimum level is a shame.

Growing up in a family with parents susceptible to hypertension; my father experiencing rheumatic fever as young man and right throughout his life, with an irregular heartbeat with his family history of high blood pressure and later diabetes filtering into the family, and my mother's side being also susceptible to high blood pressure or hypertension in the blood lines, I guess at the end of the day I am at risk of forthcoming, long-term high blood pressure and hypertension and cardiovascular issues or ischemic heart disease. But having said that, both my parents were active people and even though my dad had rheumatic fever it didn't stop him playing and being regularly active with his sports interests and being physical when it was required to do a hard day's work of digging and shovelling in the back yard.

I recall very well in late 1980 my father was hit in the chest with a cricket ball while practising in the cricket nets. At that stage he was 38 years old. This impacted on him dramatically I believe, he was ill for some time, many months actually, after that. During that period he was off work, the injury to his chest created further complications to his irregular heart beat issues and medication was required to heal it bring the heart back into some form of normality. He was on that medication for the remainder of his life. It was as if he took a bullet that day when he was hit in the heart. It was a most freakish accident, and I also feel a lot of changes began for him then too, and into the future. He lost some of his fun, his vibrancy, and whether he did or did not recover from this body trauma, I guess emotionally and physically he may have drawn caution to his levels of activity or his approach to the future, to how he viewed life. I did speak to him on occasions since that event up until his passing in 2017 of the cricket ball incident, and he said it 'shook him up and it stopped him dead in his tracks immediately'.

So, I guess I need to own up myself and give you a brief rundown after the history of my parent's health challenges. I do have fluctuating high blood pressure, fluctuating weight loss and gain at times, subject to my activity and maintenance of nutritional food balance. I control it with regular physical activity, high water intake, no alcohol (I have not been a social drinker for well over 30 years) and look to get as much rest and sleep as possible to keep fresh and alert in my day to day business. So important for me to be conscious of what I am doing and taking notice of my body and how I can best overcome my health challenges before resorting to seeing the doctor, taking medication, or seeking other professional health practitioners.

I do avoid, at all times possible, the idea of using medication as I am still not sure of its value physiologically, what it is doing to the body, how my body would react in taking medication and what I will be lead to believe it will fix. Should I invest in getting to the root cause of my illness when it comes to the surface, or really is medication serving us positively at the end of the day? Looking back on my parent's experience and their health outcomes, I guess I was curious and inquisitive, but mindful of how prescribed medication affects us and its role in the overall health to both our bodies, and general functioning as a human being.

These days at 55 years old, I am still active. I still umpire community football at a good level the Perth Football League Competition, and still play my cricket in the summer. I do a couple of community fun runs a year and have in the past ran a few half marathons. Fortunately, I have an active son who enjoys running and keeping fit, and this inspires me to also join him as much as possible in running together in fun runs.

I see that keeping active, keeping the weight down, being a non-smoker, a non-drinker and trying to be mindful of the foods I eat, is at least giving myself that chance to enjoy life with quality. I am by no means a saint, as you will find out later in this book. I can be easily swayed by my sweet tooth. Currently 1 am not experiencing any joint or muscular pain, although there are slight arthritis and inflammation indicators, but I feel that moving is the best form of treatment, along with drinking plenty of water and reducing sugars and starch in my diet. These are key areas for me to enjoying life with fun and vitality, along with working towards a less stressful mind.

At the end of the day, I am still at considerable risk of further complications to other pre-illnesses barring cardio vascular, kidney disease, diabetes etc. Both my parents have now since passed, my mother died of bowel cancer in 2005 and my father died in 2017 of prostate cancer.

So I ask the question, was my parent's illness and their passing caused by an impact on their health status, which was accumulated throughout their life's journey? What is the future for me then, my son and only son, and his future family health? Given there is a history of illness, is it time for me to take responsibility and lead the way for my son, my family, the community and the workplace community, to look at health with a different approach, of habit and behaviour change, or shall I just say it's part of the community DNA now, we all have it and blame someone else for our health status? By changing the course of my own health to a new prosperous journey and then encourage others that there is another way to enjoy life with health, and that is, by taking responsibility and not relying on others?

In the business world we are all caught up in our journeys, professions, family life, social aspects and not really taking hold of our health but looking for a masking process to make us better and not dig down and help ourselves get well again. I will delve more as we progress throughout this book.

In 2014 I finished studies in Musculoskeletal Therapy which is a study of Bio Mechanical balance correction of the body muscular system for people management of pain and general wellness. Shortly after my studies and training, I set up a Myopractic

- Kinesiologist business/practice along with Kinesiologist specialist Denise Lyon at Malaga, Western Australia. But due to personal changes and other interests of focus in my life in the beginning of 2016, I decided to move to Broome, Western Australia, where I accepted an opportunity to work as a sessional lecturer delivering health units for the Notre Dame University and this is where my thirst for research and gathering of information started me on the road to writing this book.

Prior to beginning my studies, I had performed a wide range of occupations over a 35 year or so period, from security risk management for near on 15 years, to banking, and the travel industry. I had a labour Hire and nationally Registered Training Organisation (RTO) in the late nineties and early 2000s, started delivering Human Behaviour Excellence programs and have continued since. I ventured into other areas of delivery in the Civil and Construction for a couple of years. Once again to gather experience and skill learning base to enhance my array of understanding of industries. Predominantly working on a number of Mines Sites in Western Australia, delivering heavy machinery training for a National RTO company, and throughout that period really started to make my first observations of the state of our workforce and the health associated with it.

Living and working on Mines Sites is a perfect example of life styles that are challenging in many ways. In a later chapter I will endeavour to break down the lifestyle as best as possible to give you an idea of the challenges to working and living away from home and its impacts.

But before I move forward and explain where my inquisitive mind for the future of people and their health would take me, I want to let you know I did study, and under supervision, for one year in Naturopathy in 2013 at a training and holistic clinic south of Perth. As I was completing my studies as a Myopractor, I decided to take on the extra studies in Naturopathy for one year in understanding herbal, tinctures, methods and general natural therapies practice theories and skills development, to working with patients and their pain management, and understanding the issues connecting anatomy and physiology they were experiencing, and how best to progress them to a wellness state.

The opportunity to work in a Naturopathy clinic south of Perth, studying the units, being assigned clients for five hours a week, monitoring their health, viewing their current health status and family history and discussing further treatment plans, was most enlightening for me. I thought, how lucky I am, to witness the challenges people go through and where I could assist in their wellness development. The exposure to Naturopathy gave me an insight into other forms of health practices that impressed me, and it was coming from a nature and natural approach to living, knowing that our bodies can heal itself. If there was one thing, I took from working or studying at a Naturopathy clinic, it was that our bodies are a healing machine.

In all of my life I never consciously considered my body as being a healing machine. Understanding this was like being hit by a bolt of lightning. The fact is that we can heal our bodies by changing our lifestyles for the better, giving our bodies the chance to repair itself. In the cases I witnessed first-hand working in a naturopathy clinic, I did see people's lives change for the better when they took responsibility and made lifestyle changes, not just through naturopathy medicines and approaches, but deciding to change their behaviours and habits. It was most extraordinary.

As previously mentioned in 2016, I was fortunate enough to work at the Notre Dame University in Broome, Western Australia, as a sessional lecturer and as an assessor in health studies. The students I was involved with were doing a range of qualifications from Certificate II and III in Health Studies to Diploma Level of Health Students in their first and second year of nursing studies. It was through the work I was performing at Notre Dame and through my personal research; meeting the people of the Kimberley region community, visiting towns across the Kimberley region, meeting medical professionals and leading researchers into health and progress in the area, that it became apparent to me this whole community was doing it tough not only health wise, but also emotionally and physically.

On one occasion I was fortunate enough to work for a day with a leading Broome District Hospital, Paediatrics, Doctors, nurses, and nursing assistance, to understand their health challenges and which patients were at risk and what treatment was going to be implemented for that day. I must stress that Broome is not just an Indigenous community, it embraces many diverse cultures, but the community of Broome fluctuates from 15, 000 to 20,000 people throughout the year due to its seasonal work and trade. The remainder of the Kimberley region is made up of many diverse backgrounds with 50 percent of the region being Aboriginal people.

The witnessing of, and hearing the specialists meet in the morning, talking about treatment and forms of medication to be used, and the care to be administered was an eye opener to our health status. Broome is like a lot of community towns and cities in Australia. There are issues going on and when it comes to health, it all comes to the surface and in a lot of cases, it also brings a behavioural response as well. I will chat more about our behavioural responses in one of the later chapters, how I feel there is a connection with our health and behaviour.

So, let us get back to what I am concerned about. Currently our working environment is being challenged and has done so for many working generations, which has caused an incredible amount of pain and hurt in many forms, both emotionally and physically to our bodies. When we look as far back as the Agriculture Age, then the Industrial Age, the Information Technology Age and now we are into the Conceptual Age or Creative Intensification Age, our workplace has changed. The employing and conducting of business has changed somewhat, in fact it's been overhauled on many occasions throughout the history of labour work and including office work. There have been technology changes, automative tools implemented, robots and remote controls introduced in the workplace that have affected the workplace in reduction of staff, fingertips devices that do away with having people, our communications for connecting in uncountable ways. All have moved incredibly fast, and the list goes on. But in there are people, who are going to work unwell, have chronic illnesses that include arthritis, cardiovascular complications, diabetes, kidney disease, rapid increase of obesity with forms of cancer, depression, suffering bipolar, ADHD and with that, taking medication to get through the day. Additionally there is the stress of personal issues and in many cases, dealing with other associated problems in the workplace with bullying, aggression and personal dramas. What is this doing to our own personal potential to perform, and what affects does it have to our quality of life?

I cannot explain why I ended up studying and researching in the health field, when looking back on my earlier working life. I guess after being an employee at some stage, employer, and now a business owner, I still have a great urge to make a positive contribution to improving workplace wellbeing which is now in some form of crisis. Writing this book is a way to waking up the world and saying we have only one life, let's enjoy it. We didn't get to choose our names, our parents or our date of births, but we are sure here now, so what is your aim and why wouldn't it be great to enjoy it and hopefully, a little pain free?

These days I deliver short training sessions on Human Behaviour Excellence programs, and to business networking groups on raising awareness of our behavioural responses to the workplace, and the effects of future chronic illness and its impacts to the business world. It is a passion of mine to raise the alarm that where we work impacts on our health in the long term, influenced by behaviour that eventually affects our future and quality of life.

Over the following pages I hope that I can bring you along, your family, and others with you, to having a great life. Let us give great thought to ourselves and our health. If we do then we get to have wonderful and memorable experiences, that hopefully is shared with our loved ones, work colleagues, the community and for future generations. I hope you enjoy the rest of the book and I look forward to hearing from you.

Best regards - **Greg Bridge**

Living with Chronic Illness in the Workplace

An unwell workplace

Our workplace, for the duration of its labour history of more than 120 years, has indicated and accumulated evidence of un-wellness. Through our reported or recorded accidents, incidents, injuries, trauma, emotional response, i.e., to mental health with stress, depression, and physical impairment outcomes, along with evidence of disabilities, have been on the rise ever since the beginning which has been a huge cost and burden to our community and support agencies.

It doesn't matter who we are, where we come from or what our status is in the community, we are all vulnerable to our health and becoming unwell if we are not taking care of ourselves. Our health outcomes may be a result of various forms of our lifestyle choices, genetic connections, behaviours, our environment, stresses, our nutritional value, and our naivety to our personal response to our health. In Australia, our workforce is being challenged or under siege from all forms of chronic illness, mental illness, physical disabilities, and our behaviours that are either negative or positive that influence how we look after our bodies. The costs to our health insurance and premiums rising, our public health systems costing the tax payers, the ongoing medical research and other forms of added and hidden costs are now driving our national expenditure upwards dramatically.

In Australian Health 2018, a report prepared for the Australian Government in conjunction with the Australian Institute of Health and Welfare, our overall expenditure to all health costs in 2015/16 was around 170 Billion dollars. Those costs were associated with goods and services provided by hospitals, health professions, primary care providers, and that includes general practitioners and other health professionals. We can also add to that figure the other individuals and non-government funders which include private insurers, as a part of the associated costs to our yearly health expenditure. And not to forget that our population has also increased over the last five years and is part of increasing costs to our health system.

Now, where is our working life in all this? At the end of the day, we are looking to live a positive and vibrant quality of life for our loved ones, our partners, children, grandchildren, and family members.

Our workplace is an environment with which we will be associated for a long time. It will consume, for most of us, between 33 to 40% of our lives. This in itself takes on all forms of stress, from the commitment to getting up out of bed each day, to pushing ourselves to the limit. The workplace alone has it challenges with the changing of our national and global markets. Our jobs have become more reinvented now with businesses changing their focus, the restructuring of companies and downsizing of industries, and this has now added more stress and uncertainty to the workplace. Our life of planning and designing our own futures is now at a knife's edge, which places our future and our employment opportunities in jeopardy. I will go more in depth with this later in this book, but I believe it all has relevant factors to our future wellbeing and outcomes.

Our workplace is seeing, and has done so for many years, a rapid climb in chronic illness. But now mental illness is getting more traction for impacting our workplace. In more recent times, the rise of the peripheral illnesses of depression, anxiety disorders, stress disorders and behavioural disorders contribute to compounding our workplace issues. We are also seeing the added contributing health and behavioural issues such as bullying, aggression, and injuries from assaults on site of the workplace. We also have other associated influences such as illegal drug use and substances that are having a dramatic affect. It's like there is a trigger and we have not addressed it personally, or more to the point, we have ignored it saying, it's all good, nothing is wrong, there is nothing going on.

Our health status in the workplace is struggling and we are seeing the increase of medication, poor nutritional intake, reduction of active lifestyle, smoking (but on the decline), alcohol intake on the increase and foods we are eating more processed. So, what is the end result we are looking for to our own health outcomes then?

In this book I would like to bring to attention and encourage people that chronic illness and possible other illnesses as discussed is preventable along with other contributing factors to our workplace. If we can be open to personal changes or shifts to our thinking, along with behaviours, and bring our place of work into some form of balance, enjoyment and vitality, then this is the starting point to recovery. The fun and/or enjoyment in the workplace has diminished, and I for one have seen that take place more over the last 15 or so years. When you have a workplace that loses its fun and enjoyment, then productivity and output is affected. When the workforce starts to lose its way, its direction, along with other issues of non-productivity or of dissatisfaction plus underlying stresses, begins to breakdown our good health.

In Australia right now, chronic illness is the main cause of death. It is estimated that 7 out of 10 deaths in Australia is from chronic illness or related disease or cancers. The latest statistics came out in the Australia's Health 2018, by the Australians Government body – Australian Institute of Health and Welfare. When you stand back from these statistics and look at it long and hard, it tells us that we are not in a positive state. With the rise of cardiovascular/heart disease, diabetes, kidney disease, respiratory illness, cancers, musculoskeletal, and not to mention the increase of mental illness, ADHD, multiple sclerosis, bipolar, dementia, and sleep apnoea just to add a few, our community is suffering very badly both emotionally and physically. The leading cause of deaths in Australia, for both men and women, is also from the same report of Australia's Health 2018.

So now, in relation to our currency of health in the workplace, what is the snap shot? Statistics from Medibank Private and HBF reports over the past couple of years outline common trends of information that are most disturbing to our future outcomes. We also have other health providers who have gathered similar data and information, who have been able to identify and support the trends for chronic illness and their outcomes with their members. And this is that we have 40% of the workforce aged between 25 years to 64 years of age on one form of medication dealing with chronic illness, and that they are most likely to have their chronic illness and other associated illnesses for 10 years or more.

The other concern is that it is estimated that our total workforce, or 85% of workforce, is on one form of medication and that 72% of the workforce is on two or more forms of prescribed medications. That's staggering if that is the case. So what does our workplace look like, when people are trying to just function, let alone get up out of bed in the morning to go to work when they are on either low or high dosages of medication and not feeling well? Who at the end of the day is responsible for all this? I guess looking from the outside in, everyone. We all must take responsibility for our own health primarily. Consider if the lifestyle we live, consuming substances that may not be in the best interests to our recovery or body, is serving us a good quality of life. I don't have the expertise or the knowledge in prescribed medication or other substances to know how it's affecting us or whether it's doing something of value for us. I, for one, am not questioning the medical advice for our prescribing of medication, but more so, if we as individuals need to take the lead and take hold of our health issues before it grabs a hold of us?

We have in our community, state of the art health scientists and medical researchers and advanced technologies to assess and make decisions for the betterment of our health. We have doctors and health services, but I also feel as individuals we need to work alongside our health expertise, to look to improving our own lives, use more of a preventative approach, and then continue to manage ourselves more productively and wisely. Further to that we are seeing an uprising in our responsiveness to poor behaviour, aggression, high absenteeism, mental health issues, bullying, assaults, and many more to mention with no positive or meaningful outcomes in the workplace.

At the end of the day, a huge cost in many ways to our government and public and private health systems, and to the community. Our workplace in most cases is in a state of un-wellness and we now must look at how we can turn it around to get our environment back.

Are there other contributing factors to our poor health outcomes that are progressively taking hold in the workplace? We do know our working requirements have changed over the last 10 to 20 years, we are seeing more workplaces with split shits, modified and alternative contractual employment arrangements, more or less hours required at work in some cases, more people working Saturdays and Sundays, Fly In and Fly Out work, increase in personal work performance requirements, and businesses now looking to increase their businesses to other countries of the world. This brings fantastic opportunity but further high demands on people to perform, and business to meet contractual obligations to stay competitive and be in demand. So yes, our workplace has changed, the employment conditions of employees have changed (with further conditions attached), businesses are now looking from an operational perspective on their costs, their fees, and how they can create change fast to stay in the market place. All this puts stress and uncertainty into the working community. Underpinning the above more in detail, I will raise in a later chapter the areas of change and how that has affected us with workplace health risks.

The demands in the workplace to perform our roles and duties is now ever more required. We have the added issues of toxic environments which cause great concerns to business growth, reputation, image, and internal profile, and has the business or company brought that on itself I ask? But these are all related to the employee too. Employees need to feel valued, supported and respected, and when this does not occur, the issues of not enjoying their work starts to deteriorate in many areas of a person's working life. The way people are managed and supervised has been an area of great concern for employee wellbeing and outcomes in the past, and there are many situations in my own working life, like yours, where you have examples of this.

CEO's, Managers, Supervisors and Leading Hands, have a great responsibility in working with and supporting their staff, not only in their duties but also mindful of the stresses and pressures, strain, and the overall health and wellbeing of their employees. It is clear to me that a new form of leadership now must take place in the workplace with keeping health in mind. It's not always about reporting on an individual employee's performance with their competency work ethics, but more about paying attention to their people and harnessing good will in the workplace. If we work towards a good will approach, great relationships and long term outcomes surface. Our priority is always to inspire those around us, make them feel they are valued, can have input, feedback, and solutions to issues whereby the company and employees grow and develop positively into the future. Without an inclusive workforce, the challenges are still there and once again the health of people in the workplace are challenged. They start to lose their high self-esteem and if they feel these experiences, they then lose their drive and enthusiasm to working and, in most cases, their health will start to fall away. Just remember that when people come to work, this may be the only time in their life they can shine, feel as though they are doing something worthwhile and contributing to leaving a legacy of their work behind.

This also goes for our younger generations; they need to feel part of the contribution and of being valued. They have great ideas, in some ways, to even solving our workplace issues. For a happy workforce we need to have people enjoy being part of their work, and in a lot of cases, everyone has made a huge commitment to upskilling themselves and building their expertise, their strengths and talent, and making a commitment to working in their chosen place of work and career. This goes a great way to keeping your staff happy, healthy at work, and not consider having time off.

People, when in the workplace, are reluctant at times to voice their concerns, feeling they will be ostracised, feeling that if they say something it may not be well received and they will be squeezed out of the workplace. With the increase of stress and strain and then the early onset of emotional challenges, they start to lose their productivity, focus and desire to work at their optimum level. In the years I worked for formal organisations, I came to see that there are two layers in a company. First or the top layer, as I call it, is the Fear, Ego and Control. The second layer is of Secrets, Lies and Betrayal. When these are displayed in the workplace or with intent to push people, some great avalanches appear of workplace un-wellness and people becoming vulnerable and more stressed.

Those two layers just mentioned, to me, were one of the more subtle approaches businesses and companies, managers and frontline supervisors use. These are all forms of bullying and aggression. One of the stresses I saw that people had taken on was in the area of consistencies. People view consistencies in the workplace tremendously, in fact with high regard. When consistencies are broken, trust and value fall aside and it starts to affect health, both in the short and long term. People or employees don't respond too well when there are inconsistencies in the workplace, when a company portrays to the outside world the values of their mission statement, and then they see people in high positions in their company doing and telling others to do differently and getting away with it. It's just not in the spirit of the workplace.

As I mentioned earlier, there is a connection between our health and our response to behaviour. At the end of the day it will come to the surface in some form. The high increase of workplace absenteeism, along with our work overload, the emotional challenges, poor communication skills, bullying, and aggression, is certainly on the increase. WorkSafe WA (Western Australia) have been checking this form of data for the past five years, and they have said, 'There has been a 25% increase in aggression and bullying in the workplace' assault incidents that have involved the police and lawyers. What sort of impact does that have on our health, the progression to mental health issues, which are on the rise that leads to chronic illness? It is rarely or sparingly discussed in the workplace. It is a major concern to discuss health issues, as it forms some of our underlying problems for people and their future wellbeing. When it all adds up, chronic illness connects with mental health in the workplace, and the outcomes are showing us that there is a reason for us to be concerned about the future.

Companies are more focussed on goals, targets, key performance indicators (KPI's), production and taking care of their investors, rather than looking after their most valuable resource, and this is their employees. We are all aware that it takes many people to contribute to business development growth with the modern-day pressure of still being in the market place. But a drive to focus continual respect and an inclusive approach for everyone in a company whether they be an investor, or on the front line should be valued, supported, and encouraged equally. This in turns brings great empowerment and ownership to success all round. Our employees need to feel important and this in turn creates the opportunity to have long term trusted employees who stay well and healthy throughout their employment. When we invest in each other and encourage change and awareness to health improvement in the workplace, we will start to see flourishment and so everyone wins. How great would that be, that we all involve ourselves in helping each other succeed in our future health, and then the quality of our life then flows on to embracing a balanced lifestyle with great anticipation of having a long life in the future.

Once upon a time we had one or two generations of family members in the workplace. With the increase of our working age, and now the increase of generations, we could see three and four generations of a family working for one company. Never in the history of the labour market have we seen five or six generations in the workplace. From the beginning of the Industrial Age in the late 1800s to now the Conceptual Age or Creative Intensification Age as we are currently moving into, we have many generations who are working with us. Older generations are quite different from us, they see differences in values and ideals to life aspirations, work ethics and work balance. In another time, I would place more focus on the characteristics of each generation in the workplace and how they view the world and see every one of us.

Now, given that we have an increase of generations in the workplace, what is the short and long-term health and wellness outlook moving forward? Statistically and by observance we are still in the same place. More people are joining the workforce and more compacting health issues we face continue to go forward. The rise in obesity and mental health is gaining momentum drastically in our workplace generations. With 32.2 billion dollars of business costs to Australian business in 2017 in absenteeism alone, it seems we are not slowing down. So, what do we do? Great question. Another great question is, what's the future for the workplace for businesses and employees for the next 5, 10, 20 or 30 years? What costs are going to be incurred with an ever-increasing population in Australia? In Australia, we are facing health uncertainties and then inflicting them onto the workplace with more rises in chronic illnesses, cancer, obesity, and mental health, all leading the charge along with others. Is this a problem for the government and its services to overcome, and is it able to overcome these challenges? Is this a problem for the business world to become involved in, or is it time for us as individuals to take charge of our own life and health?

Later in the book I will raise suggestions and ideas to get our minds thinking outside the square. At some point I believe we must take greater and personal responsibilities for our health and wellbeing. It is our own body, we have one life, so what are we going to do to ensure we enjoy an improved life, and also inspire those around us to having a great life of enjoyment and fun while contributing to our professions?

'When we invest in each other and encourage change and awareness to health improvement in the workplace, we will start to see people flourish, and so everyone wins'

What is Chronic Illness?

An overview

As this book is about chronic Illnesses and other related illnesses that impact our workplace community, it would be only fair to give you an understanding of how it impacts on our health and wellness. One of the interesting points I picked up even when I studied Naturopathy for 12 months, was the lecturer pointing out to our class that our body is a 'healing machine'. I must be honest with you as I mentioned previously in the opening introduction, I had never given any thought to my body being a healing machine during my early years. As a young person growing up in the sixties and seventies with my family, little was discussed about our body and how it worked, what the systems of the body were and what issues would affect your body. We were all told to visit the doctor to get a prescription or for them to tell you what the problem was and what should be done to fix it.

Little was discussed about our bodies and how we should look after it from our early years till later in life. This has now changed with modern internet, journals, and regular information on social media. People have become savvier to obtaining information to help us before we visit the doctor in what we are experiencing and then how to move forward from there.

It was from that moment and the light bulb experience, that I realised our body IS a healing machine. I became fascinated in the understanding of our body and how it worked. I looked at what I could do to my existing health challenges and what came after that to overcoming illnesses and troubles to my health. I guess being more observant, listening to myself or even paying attention to my body either internally or externally, and visually observing my state of health was the first point of reference to begin working through my issues. Along with having studied Musculoskeletal Therapy or Myopractic, relating to the balance of the body posture and structure and its effects on the body, to muscular and joint response and through body muscular adjustments, it fascinated me to how we could reduce pain and discomfort for people. Not only balancing the body, but through correcting the structure of the body to be aligned from skull, down to the base of the feet or lower limb regions.

But before I discuss some of the common chronic issues, let me give you a short health education into the 11 human systems of the body and how they interact with each other and how that connects with chronic illnesses.

The following is a list of systems that relate to our organs and functions of the body. They work in conjunction with each other and have specific functions to ensure we live, breath and have quality of life. As you look through the list of the eleven systems, I am sure you will be familiar with some of them, and possibly all of them. I have also outlined a very brief note to each of those systems and the areas of illnesses, and how they may affect our health.

1. Integumentary

2. Skeletal

3. Muscular

4. Circulatory (or better known as Cardiovascular)

5. Endocrine

6. Lymphatic

7. Digestive

8. Respiratory

9. Urinary

10. Reproductive

11. Nervous

The following are short, simple explanations of each of the body systems and what their functions are:

Integumentary - It is seen as the largest organ in the body, it's the layer of skin that covers our whole body. It is there to protect the body from the environment, from injury and infection, and stores our fat cells. Visual parts of the Integumentary system would be hair, nails, and skin. Issues such as dermatitis, rashes, skin cancer and any issue that become visible.

Skeletal – It's primarily to provide mechanical support to the body, supports the body, stores minerals, produces red blood cells to body parts including cartilage and bones, and works in association with your muscles to help you move. There are 206 bones in your body.

Muscular – It enables the movement and posture correction of the body with balance, and the muscular process of contraction and extension of the skeletal muscles in movement. It creates elasticity to allow us to move extremely fast, i.e. playing sport, running, or exercising.

Cardiovascular – It provides the transport of nutrients, gases, hormones and waste, to and from the cells of the body along with functioning with the heart and blood vessels. Pumps blood through the heart, out through the arteries, in the veins and back to the heart.

Endocrine – Secretes hormones into the bloodstream for the regulation of bodily activities. Most common notation of the Endocrine system are the glands that include the thymus, thyroid, pituitary and gonads or even male testicles.

Lymphatic – It's primarily there to protect from infectious disease to flush out. Like the endocrine system, there are glands that assist in the Lymphatic such as the thymus, lymph nodes, lymphatic vessels, and spleen region. There are common diseases such as Hodgkin's Lymphoma - a type of cancer, lymphangitis, which is inflammation of lymph muscles with swelling, elephantiasis swelling or inflammation around the ankles, just to name a few.

Digestive - It is to ingest food and break it down so it can be absorbed into the body. Most common parts are the oesophagus, stomach, liver pancreas, gallbladder, and the small and large intestines.

Respiratory – This enables gases to exchange, supply the blood with oxygen and remove carbon dioxide from the lung region. Areas to supporting the respiratory function include the trachea, bronchi, and lungs.

Urinary – This enables liquid waste from the body and it is also to regulate water balance. Organs associated to this system's functions include the kidney, ureter, bladder, and the urethra. One of those examples would be where kidney stones have started to form, which makes life a bit uncomfortable and unbearable if you have had them, but they will pass through with time. Ensure to drink plenty of water or otherwise seek medical attention.

Reproductive – (female and male) Female, produces eggs and supports the new developing foetus or offspring. Organs associated to the female include ovary, uterus, cervix and vagina. Male – produces and delivers sperm and associated fluids, associated parts of the male include prostate, testicles, and the penis.

Nervous – It is a sensory function which communicates with other parts of the body such as the brain, spinal cord, and nervous system. A most intricate system, especially in the first stages of the embryo or foetal stage of the development of the new born. If issues arise, impairments neurologically start to happen with long term chronic illness or even cognitive behaviours that affects the learning and ability for a new born child to develop their function for later in their life.

All the above are basic systems of the human body. They all interlock and work with one another to keep our body system in a balanced function. Any form of breakdown in these areas of illness can start the slow process to a pre-illness then onto a possible chronic illness. You may have heard of 'Acute' which relates to early stages of pain that occurs over a brief period of 48 hours then may go away. You may need a specialist to help in the management or surgical requirements to overcoming the issues. Whereas, 'Chronic' pain or illness is over an extended period, or for the rest of your life or long-term condition as it is experienced.

I would encourage people to further investigate and understand how their body functions work. Just to be aware of its role. It is your job to take care of your body and understanding how it works would be of great advantage to you.

We also need to also encourage our younger generations to become more aware of their body and its functions. The workplace should also be a place to discuss and bring up information and awareness to health trends that would make a difference to their environment and be part of business development strategies to improving wellness for everyone. There are many information packs, free services and agencies who would be extremely glad to attend your place of work and share tips and strategies to improving the workplace. Most important to help our workplace and work colleagues, and how we can overcome and prevent the health challenges in the workplace. With modern day information circulating through the internet, and other vehicles to keep you up to date with knowledge in the anatomy and physiology area.

As discussed in chapter one, chronic illness makes up for 7 out of 10 deaths in Australia. This statistic also on a par with the rest of our world countries and population. Chronic illness is preventable in a lot of cases, but unless we find the issues and the treatment to overcoming them, we are all facing the possibilities of chronic illness taking our lives at some stage in the future, if we don't immediately change our behaviour to living a balance life style.

Just to give you a more defined explanation of chronic illness or condition, it is a human condition or a disease that persists over a longer period of time or comes over a period of more than three months or more.

There are other chronic diseases that you are more commonly aware of, such as coronary or heart disease in which obesity contributes, diabetes, arthritis, cancer, viral diseases, kidney, HIV/AIDS, Multiple Sclerosis, as such, we will cover them in later chapters in more depth. An illness over a longer period can coincide with a terminal illness that leads to death.

In the work I have performed in studying to be a Myopractor, our primary focus was always to firstly assess the body and posture structure. The most common problems experienced when coming into my practice were lower lumber stillness and soreness of muscular issues, cervical or lower neck pains, hamstrings from sports related complaints, collapsed arches in the feet, headaches, sciatica leg complaints, and short leg syndrome. Migraines were the most common areas of client complaints. As a Myopractor, you're looking to balance the body for correction, with the hope that you reduce pain. This has a top down affect to the mid line of the body.

Myopractic practitioners do a range of other treatments. From muscular adjustments, giving information with regards to nutritional management, to stretching and looking at our lifestyle approach to continual health. One of the areas I felt was necessary was on the emotional side of our health and musculoskeletal system. Our emotional state to wellness is critical to our health outcomes. I felt in a lot of cases the assessment in muscular response when signs showed non-improvement, that other things were impacting the person responding to wellness. Just maybe, they are experiencing other forms of challenges such as their emotional state that was stopping them from healing back to good health.

An example of this was back in 2014. I was seeing a patient called Susan for a couple of weeks. I was not really getting the muscular response correction I needed to work her body back into balance. Susan was displaying very tight quads and hips that were not flexing enough to get a range of motion in the required degrees. She was not able to get a flex, and her biggest challenge was that I couldn't assess her movements of her legs and hips to get a response. She was having great difficulties in hips rotating back to normal position. After her third appointment, and still not getting the response I was looking for, I then started to ask Susan questions. If at any time I am not achieving early results, I would say to the person I am not progressing well enough or as effective as I would like to be, and then look at what alternative approaches we could take. Possibly, let's look at what other therapies could assist more greatly. After the third session I asked Susan a couple of questions as my curiosity was starting to pique. What was going on in her life, how was she feeling, was she enjoying life, was there unnecessary stress, how was her home life, just really to break the ice and see if there was an emotional issue that was preventing her body back to wellbeing.

It was during that third session she opened up and informed me that her intimate life with her husband had taken a nose dive, as she and her husband were unable to have frequent sexual intercourse. Digging down a little deeper with Susan revealed that her frustrations and belief systems of her quest to enjoy a sexual experience with her husband went back further, well before they were married. It turned out that when she was around five years of age up until 12, she was sexually molested and badly mistreated. She felt she was not worthy of a good life or a good husband (which she had married). Her husband treasured her, as they had three children along the way in their married lives together. But this early experience, and now not enjoying active sexual pleasure, was impacting on her psychologically. She also explained that she was always feeling guilty for not being able to firstly enjoy sexual intimacy, and that she felt she had let her husband down at the same time. She was carrying the burden of the past and it was having great effects on her overall self-esteem in life. Once we brought that out and looked at where we could go from there and not feel judged at the same time, she set herself on the road to clearing her thoughts, emotions, and responses to those early experiences.

We did it with the help of a counsellor, and Susan was able to clear some of the unwanted and emotional baggage from the past and she is still working through it, but with more non-judgement and with self-relief.

Once we looked at the possible avenues for Susan to regather or reclaim herself, she then came back to my practice and we were able to correct her posture and now enjoys a more positive and less stressful life with her family and society. Emotional blockage in a lot way plays a huge in part in people's recovery back to good health. We should not underestimate that process of emotional wellness, when and if we identify it, and if you push through it you will see great personal results and self-relief. In most cases you will end up healing yourself and regaining your self-esteem. When you consider our bodies and how it reacts to events, injuries, personal trauma, the environment, our nutritional intake, consumption of tobacco and alcohol, then to stress and other substances i.e. medication of illegal substances, we put ourselves through great personal challenges. In most cases we are not conscious of our doings and any thought to the outcomes of our habits or traits are dismissed. We take for granted our bodies function and what we are doing throughout the process. It's the only one we will get during our life, so let's look after it.

The following scenario is yet another example of where the emotional state was interfering with someone showing signs of inflammation or swelling, while I was palpating the cervical or lower neck region of the body.

In this case I had a new client in Phil, age 64, medium build, in a married relationship of 40 years, had a secure job for his age, kept active but was a little on the overweight size, who initially came to me with neck pains. He did have slight issues to the lumber region with pains, which we corrected and he was able to get on with life and enjoy his physical work. During the first visit of assessment he displayed on his back, the upper thoracic area near the base of the neck or cervical region, a huge amount of swelling. This is common in the work I perform, to see swelling in the lower cervical or posterior neck region. It looks very much like a cyst or a knot of tissues but with fluid formation. When I was palpating just below the cervical 1 vertebra, an area of concern as I was pressing down on Phil's back, felt like fluid of inflammation. It was clear to me that there was something going on more than an injury or a trauma to his body. Like with Susan, I discussed the issues with Phil, soon after the first session. I began to ask him questions to see if there was a way of finding the underlying cause of his inflammation.

It turned out that he had grown up in a violent and controlled home environment. He was always afraid to say 'no', but to say 'yes', otherwise he would receive a belting or be sent to his room as a young child. He expressed to me that whenever he makes a decision in his working life or makes a decision with people at work, he always has this feeling of apprehension, and was looking for that next moment he would be told off. But he did say he went through life with constant 'nodding of the head' in saying yes, all the time, but couldn't say no in fear of being chastised or spoken to aggressively.

This type of scenario is in our community more than we think. I am not saying that everyone with fluid retention or inflammation is all due to the emotional response to our feelings, or the past, but there must be a connection to assisting ourselves back to wellness. Not just through therapy for an injury to the body, an accident, or a physical response, sure they have an influence, but it's the healing of the body that matters. The body is a healing machine, and if there are situations of emotional issues blocking the recovery, could that also play a role in overcoming our health and illnesses?

With people like Phil and Susan, who have taken on personal misjudgement, trauma, treated badly as young people and abused, their emotional responses are shattered. Their health issues escalated from acute to long term chronic through stress, low self-esteem, poor resistance to regaining their wellness, unhappy lives, always trying to prove to people their worth and value in the community, looking to establish their place in society, and now having to deal with, and work through their experiences of the past. When your past events are not addressed, and emotions to these events are held and not addressed, health issues will come to the surface and that could be in the form or signs of inflammation, our behaviour response when triggered. It's important to be open to our healing process, not from just a physical sense, but to our emotional situations that we are experiencing, as it all blends together, I am sure.

So, when Phil and Susan came into the work place as young people, like others you and I know of, they are already disadvantaged. Every time they do something, decide, present something to their employer or turn up for work, underneath their exterior is an emotional wreck looking to get some validation and encouragement. When the truth be known, they are struggling with their personal and past life history and then their health starts its decline. Who knows chronic illness or pre-illness has already commenced? What was really coming out for me is that we have incredibly talented and committed people around us now losing their identity and seeing their future being challenged with their health. Our emotional baggage and life experiences is just another add on to the weight we carry around with us. If we don't start to clear that, we end up becoming more ill, and that starts to impact further on our chronic illness. We start to experience other forms of illness in depression, dementia, stress, and anxiety disorders.

In 2008, I embarked on my journey to cleanse myself and to get rid of the dark cloud that was hanging over my shoulder for almost forty years. I experienced forms of misjudgement of self-belief, due to my early schooling life and youth years. I felt in the back of my mind that I was constantly being judged with most things I did. It was those years of my schooling that I took on the unnecessary stuff of not being good at school. When I did leave school, I went to work for the Commonwealth Bank, and I guess from there I was to set out to disprove my beliefs.

Since those days, I have had a most wonderful working experience as you may have read so far. It's a journey of taking on new challenges. But still I had to address the black cloud over my shoulder, and in 2008 I did that, through self-development programs which I have since developed, to aid people in the workplace to overcome their self-doubt issues and hopefully work them towards wellness. When I addressed my dark cloud other areas of my life, my health and engaging with people and family friends improved. More importantly, I learnt the value of our internal language and that is a great passion of mine, to see how we can turn that upside down and give it a new meaning. That is when I began the Dynamics of Language programs as part my Human Behaviour Excellence programs in the workplace.

Our relationships, both with ourselves and with others, is related to the outcomes of our communications, and language use is at the forefront. Our emotions do play a key role, it improves our health when we find the issues and we then give ourselves permission to work with ourselves. Remarkable results come from it.

It was clear to me in the work I was performing as a Myopractor, in muscle response and balancing of the body, that chronic illness, our emotional and our behavioural responses play a huge part in our fight for healing. Considering our workplace will be a part of us for the best part of our lives, it doesn't make sense that we are working in environments that are not conducive to good health, are poor working places and with bad behaviour dramatically increasing. A lack of modern day leadership, poor communication skills, bullying, aggression, and inconsistencies of ethics in the workplace with corporate companies and small business, show that at the end of the day people take it on and become unwell and don't look forward to getting up out of bed in the morning. In most cases people will consider moving on to another profession, another company, and will probably end up in the same environment as the last. As with most business environments, there are much the same traits, poor behaviours, and attitudes. Certainly, from my experience, that did occur on a couple of occasions and the feedback from people I have met over the past say the same thing too. Most of them end up telling me that they became ill and needed extended periods of time off from work. In a later chapter of this book I will discuss this further.

In 2014 when studying a year of Naturopathy, I was spending five hours per week being supervised in at Naturopath clinic, in Cockburn, south of Perth CBD in Western Australia. Understanding and administering alternative health therapies took on a whole new mindset for me. As part of my studies and practical work of reinforcing my knowledge and skills in the anatomy and physiology field, the understanding of basic herbal therapies was introduced. One of the more popular and common complaints people were being identified with was the issue of Irritable Bowel Syndrome or known as IBS or stomach region. In the basics of Naturopathy studies and like formal medicine studies, the concept of our body reacts to different changes and experiences. The understanding was that there were key areas to our health that if not harnessed or consciously looked after, were indeed in danger of illness. What was common with IBS seemed to be in common in my research and observation with everything else in our future health; there is a connection to chronic illness outcomes in the workplace. So, to break this down, when your environment is not settled or is unhealthy. Just to bring you up to speed, we are now seeing more businesses working from home, so the idea of work and home may play out its own challenges to our health and wellness too. All forms of reactions take place, your health deteriorates, you lose sight of your focus, you stop enjoying life, you do things that seem out of character, behaviours start to show different aspects of who you are, your energy levels start to decline, and then you start to not feel well and other illnesses start to take shape and then surface.

When stress becomes key in your reaction to personal events, your immune system starts to breakdown, you have no resistance to fighting virus and illness, you lose sleep, become anxious, angry, irrational with decision making, and this further implodes our health issues or could even trigger other health conditions not experienced before, and future internal diseases. Then when we include our nutritional diets, and if not balanced with fruits, grains, vegetables, and sea foods, our diets of high processed meats may have new reactions to our bodies. The increase of sugars in body weight, the fast rise in weight to obesity (which is now an epidemic issue in Australia), lack of exercise and activity, our vitality for life can shift from being highly active and conscious to beginning our stages towards un-wellness in the future. Then if you include our intake of alcohol and tobacco, what is it doing to our bodies?

In going back to my time at Naturopathy studies and the IBS process, it appears from the work I was performing at the Naturopath clinic, along with medical experts, the message is that IBS is critical, and in fact, it is the engine room for our body. So, what we take in must be digested and broken down, and then there is a reaction which gives an outcome. We must give great thought to what we consume in terms of what nutritional foods we ingest, for our future health.

When we combine our environment, stresses, nutritional intake, alcohol and tobacco, and not to mention medication and illegal drugs, we are only putting our body at further risks and compounding our existing illnesses. Yes, increasing our risks to health issues and creating future health complications with possible long-term illnesses that may be linked to cancers, arise. Even though we have only briefly discussed the different effects of chronic illness in our own bodies, the opportunity is here for us to consider our health and know we must take responsibility for our health. It's a shame to know that we can prevent our chronic illnesses before they start and at least before they have the chance to impact us. Everyone should be encouraged to find out more about their bodies and the potential illnesses they could face, and where they have contracted chronic illness. We spend more time investigating, resourcing, and tracking information about other goings-on in life, but not much to looking at how our bodies function and to improving our wellness in one form or another. It's time for us to do something positive for ourselves, not turn a blind eye, as we only get one chance on this earth, and many of our loved ones would have loved to live more years or even one more day. We also owe it to our spouses to keep well, be vibrant and show our children it's time to take care of themselves and then share our human spirit with the whole community. How good would that be? Just think of what that would do to our community and for us. Small health changes such as activity, our workplace environment, personal management, our lives, our nutritional approach, a bit of fresh air and taking good care our health will be the start to preventing illnesses and to allowing yourself to have a fun and enjoyable experience. I want to encourage people to enjoy their workplace and see the brilliance come from that.

'I would encourage people to further investigate and understand how their body functions work'

A Business Approach to Illnesses in the Workplace

Is it time for our workplace to consider an eco-friendly environment that provides a place of wellness, that's vibrant, inclusive, engaging, and makes efforts to reduce the stresses and strains of our work life? A place that encourages positive behaviour that values our staff and management, that inspires to bring the best out in people and their talent, and with great health and wellness in mind? We are now seeing our workplaces designed with eco-friendly buildings. It does revitalise the workplace and the individuals and is a proactive approach to how we implement change that will be of great (health and wellness) benefit to our work. Or do we continue to subject our workplace with old and tired environments that only induce a place of unhappiness and with no real enjoyment, low productivity, and filled with controlling attitudes?

Businesses right now are so focused on stamping their own brand, their territory, their service, their product without no conscious thought to their employees and the workplace environment. We know that in the modern world, competition is at a premium, that our businesses are evolving every day, and costs to services are being challenged, but without an inclusive and happy workplace, many talented people will start to suffer in many ways.

The importance in keeping your reputation, profile and image, is paramount to your ongoing success, as the window to your business invariably is your frontline staff who are the first point of contact to customers. In most cases they are the conduit to your business, and your staff member could be the best customer your business has, as per the old business practice around internal customer system approach. With a happy workplace and work force you will ride through the tough and challenging times and build strength and hopefully prosper and grow into the future. Trust is a key value to business and retention of skilled staff, not the wages you may pay them. When we acknowledge and give recognition to our workforce, they feel valued and develop a strong sense of worth. It's not always the wages that keep people working for an organisation - just simple gratitude. I guess the question I now ask is: is your workplace emotionally well and free of fear?

We have on the rise more reporting of behaviour, increasing litigation and continuing up surge of law suits, more media attention, openly social media comments or public comments, high claims on workers compensation and other reports of what is happening in the workplace. Being involved as I am in delivering the Human Behaviour Excellence programs, when I discuss with other businesses what's happening in their workplace, I get a very vague look and closed conversations. When I approach businesses and organisations of their potential to issues like bullying, aggressive behaviours, bad language use, substandard attitudes that are possibly affecting their image and reputation, most of them go underground and say nothing. It's as if companies are all holding a blank shield, it's an "area they don't want to get into", is a basic response I get. Even in the event of being in a conversation when someone asks me what I do, businesses just communicate as if there is nothing going on. But when they are challenged with an incident, and look at ways to deal with it, it turns out they didn't have policies and procedures in place to assist in overcoming their issues. We are seeing a lot of businesses not paying attention to their potential internal crisis's and wait for it to occur. They are more reactive than proactive, and this is where we start to find the issues that will hurt our workplace. Just consider if you are in business or you're an employee, what are the costs to you if you don't say something or have an issue resolved? It's costly in the end. Only you in business, or employees, will know of the behaviours and issues compounding your operations, while you are more focused on your production, bottom line, KPI's, your image, your reputation, your profile and potential, and growth of your business. It should be a focus, but businesses are also employing staff, contractors, and researchers. As mentioned earlier in chapter one, there are two layers in which I feel companies like or may not like to operate at, or subconsciously operate at: the fear, ego and control, and the other layer of secrets lies and betrayals. It's that sort of environment that when you bring in either layer, it serves no one any positive outcomes or goodwill in return. We will discuss more about workplace behaviour in Chapter 7.

So, having said that, let's look at how our health outcomes appear in all of this. A combination of behaviours and people working in silence with challenging health issues can only worsen the un-wellness in the company and individuals. A toxic workplace environment in which most of us have all experienced at some stage, who have demonstrated or displayed unethical behaviours and inconsistencies fuels fire within the company and work colleagues. I know in my time when I have worked in formal or corporate organisations, there have been many examples of unfair play, behaviours displaying poor management, and language use, with no great outcomes. In some cases, it has led to people taking on the issues personally, to then becoming ill themselves through absenteeism, reporting sick, early stages of depression, stress fatigue related responses at great costs to the company and employer, and then to possibly facing a long term away from the company. So what are the costs then?

When it comes to individuals experiencing their illnesses, they are very unlikely to mention to anyone in the workplace of their health status due to attitudes and actions the company may take on people being unfit and unwell. The mere fact that someone is struggling with an illness or a health-related issue, the employee feels that their position or job future is in jeopardy. The value one holds for their job means a great deal to their current personal situation, quality of life, their relationships, and their own personal freedom to enjoy their life. In the case of a chronic illness, it's most probably a long-term experience or indefinite. No doubt in my time in the workforce, I have seen a dramatic up-rise in stress disorders with work colleagues, with both young and older generations. I couldn't begin to know how people get through, let alone functioning through the day. To turn up for work and perform is obviously a challenge, and along with their own internal feelings makes it even harder for them to see their way through it.

People's first point of reference is to protect their livelihood and the personal commitments they have. Keeping their employment is paramount. The risk of losing their employment is most stressful in the current market place, jobs are not plentiful, safe, and at times, unpredictable in finding new work, as the work environment has shifted to causal or part time or contracting work. So working in silence is the first strategy one would employ before contemplating approaching a staff member or manager if they feel they don't have someone to speak to in confidence. In the meantime, people work through their pain and discomfort, on medication, with self-guilt for their illness, and then coping with an environment that is toxic and unpleasant. Not all places are toxic, there are companies who do an enormous amount of progression to ensure their place of work is positive for all types of activities and very inclusive for everyone to take part in, which in turn brings impressive results and outcomes for both the company and employees.

Companies should consider if not before a more inclusive and embracing culture, an open approach to people in their organisation when they are feeling challenged with a personal issue, or have a health issue, to come forward. In a lot of cases employees have been long term, loyal and have developed strong integrity-based ethics which is of immense value. If an organisation is not open to their employees approaching them with their personal or health status, then that would raise alarms bells that the fear, ego, and control is in its sights. Fear driven behaviour only drives stress, and then goes on to affect the individual or the company into a toxic and un-well state. It is an all-round outcome at the end that will only create an environment of sickness leading into the future for everyone. The emotional wellbeing of an environment, if not handled or managed, will start to impact on your image, reputation, profile, productivity, bottom line and the long term growth and rewards in the future.

Looking back during my working life and into the future, I see a new approach to leadership, with keeping health and wellness in mind. I know we have a plethora of leadership courses, training, and alternative methods to how leadership should look in an ideal world but incorporating areas of health to open the minds of the new leaders of the world is so important. New leadership styles are based on inspiring, inclusiveness, team work origins, solution driven ideals, but health should also be included. If people are not well, no one goes anywhere. Once again health, when discussed, is thrown out the door and not brought into the equation, which is the core of our existence and function to perform. I am sure as we move into the future and beyond 2020 supervisors, managers and senior management level companies will respond to the needs of the employees with a holistic approach to humanistic values.

What responsibility is it to a business and its employees in relation to health and wellness in the workplace? A shared approach is a positive approach to engaging and keeping everyone aware of our health. In recent years we have seen an increase in promotional and advertising of sensitive issues to the stop smoking campaigns and to reducing our alcohol content. Both in our community is one of the key driving points in our ongoing chronic illnesses, and to also increasing our risks for cancer and mental health, that includes depression, dementia, multiple sclerosis etc. We have all seen the outcomes of these in our community and with our loved ones and friends.

The workplace can be a challenging place most of the time with our roles, and continual performance-evaluation assessments we go through every three to six months. It is like that stigma of being at school all those years ago, another test to attend and what the outcome will be if I don't pass it. These days I don't dwell over it much, but those things do go through your mind when you have to sit down for your workplace progressive report. It is a taxing and stressful emotional moment, the importance to us keeping our jobs and having a place of work is so significant in many ways for our own future and quality of life. It just creates another form of anxiety we must deal with and in some cases, people are most stressed out by it and then must seek help to overcome it.

The hidden challenges of our illness, compounded with our social drinking if uncontrolled, and if with smoking, along with poor nutritional intake, also influence whether we are going to struggle getting up out of bed to face the day. Whether we will be in pain and emotional wrecks, not able to face the world let alone the workplace. I do know of some workplaces that are increasing their efforts to encourage good life management systems and environments for their employees as previously discussed, as we have seen the inclusions of gym facilities, a greenhouse environment approach to have people feel welcomed and engaging to work, open space working cubes, ensuring offices have adequate air supply, drinking water for access to prevent dehydration, more sunlight, designing buildings and offices to be more friendly and flexible or shared working hours. I will open up more to where businesses and the workplace are looking to move into the future in Chapter 10.

Chronic illness and its associated illnesses are costly to our community, and in a business sense it creates an indirect cost, reducing productivity and loss of work days. Through the increase in absenteeism in the workplace in Australia, it is reported to have cost businesses and government services around 32.2 billion dollars in the last year in 2017. It is staggering to think that some of those costs could be avoided by preventative life style changes and more education and information circulated to improving our workplace health. Companies also along with high absenteeism, face loss of productivity, a turnover of employees, rise in costs to their shifting business expenses in the market place to compete and impact, cost to workers compensation insurances, and other unforeseen financial business burdens.

With businesses constantly looking to improve their services and status, they are also working in a world of continuous shifting through workforce demographics. There is a challenge for companies to attract the most talented and professional employees. It's not just necessary employing people with highly decorated qualifications in the science fields, but more hands-on soft skills are going to be required in the future. Staff will go through on-going education skills improvement to stay on top of their workload and be able to create for themselves, as the X Factors of being their own unique employee. Companies are now having to expand their operations and even move their operations to other parts of the world, to be more competitive and part of the globalisation market that also creates great change and in a lot of cases, uncertainty for everyone in the workforce. The change in businesses and relocation further impacts on the stress and strain of the workforce, then on top of that impact, a pre-illness or with their existing chronic illness, and other family factors and personal issues, the confidence in keeping your job is becoming ever more so challenging. Employees are looking for sustainable jobs and now that we are seeing more flexible, contractual work, it will make it difficult in the future. But then again it will suit people who choose to work and be comfortable with flexi hours.

It is suggested that people, in the next 20 to 40 years, may have up to 30 or more jobs in their life time. Change appears to be imminent, so l say, get ready. With all this being discussed and talked about through various forms of commentators, media reports, economists, labour, and human resources experts, we may see less loyalty from the employers and employees for future business. If we have both employers and employees with similar ethics, values and purpose, that complement each other, then we will see great outcomes. But this is not always the way in a perfect world.

I would like to let you know that not all employees experience chronic illness, but we are seeing more of them becoming or playing the part of home carers to their spouses. In Australia we have seen a dramatic rise in spouses not only go to work each day, but also take the roles of carers. Having the responsibility of being an active and healthy employee and then at the same time as carers, raises continual stress and anxiety in relationships, general health, and wellbeing. Now that we are seeing more carers who are also working in the workplace, companies may need to look at their strategies to aiding their staff with supportive flexible hours and with any needs to the employee.

We are seeing more companies look to how they can help their staff and take some of the pressures off them, to have an all-round partnership approach. It is great for long term trust, morale, and good relationship sense. The responsibility of companies is to ensure their senior staff in supervisory or management roles, look to develop other skills to assist when the employee in the workplace will be needed into the future. This investment by companies to aid their staff and encourage them, will only lead to enhancing the relationships and prospering their business potential. The word will get out that a business has a comprehensive approach not only to its clients, but to its employees. Its great reputation to have.

It is without doubt that companies and small businesses will need to consider and review their policies and procedures to their workplace in the future. Considering that their business may be under threat in future, with people who are being challenged in their health and who have responsibilities to loved ones needing carers support out of the workplace.

One of the ways employers, companies and small businesses can work with employees who have responsibilities being a carer, is through flexible working hours. We are seeing businesses change their approach to doing business and with National markets in Australia and Globalization at our front door. Businesses are looking to broaden their market, and here lies the potential and increased opportunity to have flexible working hours. Market demand does drive change and flexi hours is an alternative way to do business while managing costs and effectiveness of business operations.

Flexi hours restructures the job roles for an employee and alleviates stress at work and at home. Sharing jobs may also be other alternative approach too, as we now, more than ever, must come up with an open view. We are seeing more in the return to work of women, in their quest to pick up where they left off before having children. There are increased arrangements now, whereby employees are working from home, with office equipment supplied to give that real feel for an office, and it provides the employer the opportunity to work from home and manage their responsibilities at home. Company supervisions do put their own systems in place to monitor the work load and the productivity and output of the employee in their jobs. Companies are seeing the benefits to both environments of employee and employer, to achieving the desired productivity and outcomes for all concerned.

Hours of flexibility can range in various forms from flexible hours, part time hours, hours of compound where hours are longer but reduced days in the week, for example Fly in Fly Out, or four days on and three days off one week, and then three days on and four days off or unpaid work. The relationship between employee and employer will be enhanced with an open and honest approach to producing a strategy to moving forward, that will see the support and to working with health issues if the need arises.

Companies are now considering very closely their own workplace environment to embracing the needs and support of their staff at work. This also helps people with chronic illness or experiencing un-wellness. So, redesigning the workplace is a choice. In terms of developing a workplace which is stress free, environmentally friendly, more sunlit spaces, more circulation of air, and being encouraged to drink more water, is already being introduced in many buildings in the Perth, Central Business District, in Western Australia.

The City of Perth have been, for the past five years (since 2013,) encouraging new buildings to be erected that consider an eco-friendlier approach to their completion, understanding that Perth as a city and like many cities around the world, attract a high density of working population and to consider the future wellness of people while at work. This model of approach removes barriers towards creating ill health, it is more equally supportive to people with disabilities and their enjoyment in coming to work, knowing that their workplace is eco-friendly, which in turns helps the staff to be happy as well.

Our issues with health and disabilities can be a complex relationship, and in some cases, we have people who have been on long term disabilities which may further contribute to their lingering, or future chronic illnesses, as such. It's estimated that one in five Australians have some form of disability. People will have mild or moderate core activity limitations, which in some cases will be restrictive in working in the workplace or even being able to leave their home. This becomes most frustrating and self-impacting on our wellness whether we are at work in the community, or our social scene. There are other forms of disabilities, and that leans more to the influences of our mental health issues that compound on our overall health to function and be active. Businesses are looking to embrace new employees, along with providing an environment that easy, friendly, and helps to improve people's lives with disabilities in the workplace.

This can only enhance business and companies looking to be proactive, and with employees support to building change, making a positive environmental change. Companies with strong workplace policies and support programs have the potential to be significant in the work place, with lives being valued more so. Companies are putting up new options to address their needs, and they are looking to engage with their employees towards a balanced approach. It has become clear especially when a business is operating on a global scale that everyone is in demand to perform and become more proactive. It is so important for companies to keep engaging with employees, working out solutions between them, and that the workplace is sustainable and productive.

Chronic illness or pre-illness is here to stay unfortunately, but we can also work towards preventing it too. We have an increase in mental health concerns in the workplace in Australia, and that is on the rise. The costs to an individual and the community is an alarming billions of dollars every year. Now is the time for us as individuals to take some responsibility here and see if we can claw back our lives. We are fast losing our health, our emotional state is being challenged constantly, and there is an onerous responsibility for us to look at our life style balance and being honest, are we really loving the life we live? Now that we have un-wellness in our hands, it is up to us to take a stand and lead by example for us, our families, and the community. Now is a terrific opportunity to make these personal changes in changing the world with small steps and doing so consistently.

'A place that encourages positive behaviour that values our staff and management, that inspires to bring the best out of people, their talent and with great health and wellness in mind.'

Shifting of the Workplace

Given that our workplace will take on new forms of change over the next five, ten and twenty years, what is happening now may impact in the future. Whether you are an employer, a contractor, a consultant, a student, or a researcher in various fields, the workplace has shifted dramatically. In the last chapter, I briefly mentioned the areas of challenge with people in the workplace with chronic disease and how companies are looking to redesign and encourage an inclusive workplace. One alarming comment was made by Forbes Magazine in 2013, saying that, "Work was more of a place of frustration than fulfilment for 90 percent of the world's workers". It's now 2018, but those comments by Forbes is relevant to the work and the observations I have made in the past five years. So, what is this saying about our workforce and jobs future, and what effect is this having on people in their health and stresses to not enjoying life, even before getting out of bed?

Also reported by the Gallup, global employees were more disconnected from their workplace. It was estimated at around 85 percent of the workforce in Australia, The Gallup said, 'In America, 70 percent of their workforce hated their jobs".

Considering those statistics and in reflection of the Australian workforce, there have been industry discussions and forums by State Training Councils in recent times, Government Workplace Reform Groups and Specialists in Human Resources, to decide where business and employment will be in the future. We are on par, in Australia, with what Forbes Magazine and the Gallup report about America's workplace trends. So, what does this say about our workforce and where we are likely to head into the future?

Given that we have a workforce that is experiencing personal health and emotional un-wellness, which is the key to us going to work each day, I see that we are in a crisis, along with people's own relationships and financial challenges, plus many other personal distractions they face and then trying to blend it in with a socially connective life with life balance. It becomes very tough to manage our lives. Having mentioned earlier that 85 percent of our workforce is on one form of medication and with an estimated 72 percent of the workforce on two or more medications, we are struggling in our community. With our population and diverse cultures expanding, it's increasing our future risks to our wellness and the wellness in the workplace. How will this stretch or limit people in their own self growth, and to encourage them to play a positive role in their professional future?

Businesses will need to be more conscious of where they are heading from a workforce wellness point of view, with implementing strategies and resources to manage and develop ways for their future operations.

In more recent years, we have seen Australia experiencing a down turn in the mining market and other affected industries that had been an influential part of financial momentum. With the challenges in those sectors and others, and putting strain further on the workplace environment, it has taken on a new shape. But in there lies our wellness in the workplace, and the stress of our day to day life has further increased. The workforce in some ways is feeling fatigued, with more pressure on people to perform, the restructuring of companies, and reduced labour market business causing businesses to rethink their way moving forward with possible less market share. Individual jobs are on the line causing great concerns for all parties.

One thing is for sure, when I was project managing one of the projects for the Financial Administrative Professional Services (FAPS) Training Council, Western Australia, between 2012-2014, it was clear that we are now in the age of reinventing ourselves. Training Councils in Western Australia were made up of ten of them covering industry, related to their respective Councils. In relations FAPS, it was responsible for representing Industries included in Administration, Retail, Pest

Management, Security, Cleaning, Banking, Financial and Surveying. During that period working with FAPS, I had the pleasure of working with incredible and skilled people, not only from a management but from an industry and training background. On many occasions I attended Career Expos, Skills West Weekender, Regional Training Forums, Indigenous Careers Expos, Training Councils meetings and State Training Reviews. All along it was pointing to how business and people will need to armour themselves up the future in the workplace. 'Reinventing yourself was here' and it will be in the future. The suggestion that we may, or the current and new generation workforce will have, 30 or so jobs in the future, looks most possible. The continual redevelopment of our skills and knowledge will be a requirement going forward. So, what does that say about our health and emotional state to the change taking place, because it is here, and reinventing, up skilling ourselves is ever present and will be to the end of your working life.

The uncertainty of our jobs only impacts on the stress of our current health status. There are many factors people face in going to work each day, and then having to watch their health just lowers the spirits. Our hours have increased. Gone are the nine to five jobs, some people are working more hours at work, others are having them shortened or changed to suit the employer or employee as determined by market demands. But underneath it all, people are facing a huge challenge in working with their health.

The increasing issue of jobs being made redundant, redesigned or restructured, puts people on edge. The uncertainty of where they are going causes a more sickening and anxious feeling inside that starts to set of all sorts of internal emotions, anxieties, and stress. They worry of their future, knowing someday, a manager will come to them and ask them politely to come in to their office to be then shown out. I am the first to put my hand up as I have experienced this on several occasions, and it is a mixed feeling of thoughts that goes through your head. Those that have been through this process will understand the reaction to being told you no longer have a job.

The ongoing stress of our job futures and security not only puts further strains on the increase of mental illnesses but will impact on our physical ability to be active in the workplace. Being employed and enjoying our work improves our health, protects it, instils self-esteem and gives a sense of identity and self-worth. It increases our wellness with social connection and provides the opportunity to personally develop ourselves going forward. Even if someone is challenged with their health, the chance of being employed and working is a huge advantage to getting on with, and then starting to reassess, their health goals if that is priority.

One of the jobs I can relate to as I observed, was when I was contracted to deliver training for a Registered Training Organisation in Western

Australia in Civil Engineering. Just to put you in the picture I was not initially from that industry, but having had a strong connection of past clients in that industry, and having a background in training, assessing and compliance, and with the opportunity to do something completely different and out of my comfort zone to learn and perform a new task with a new industry, was very exciting. My role was to visit various mine sites two days here, five days there and ten days here and there. Very random training projects to be delivered through Western Australia and the Northern Territory, delivering training on heavy machinery over an eighteen-month period in the mid 2000's.

What was telling there, was the life of a miner or a FIFO worker. I started to document my travels and the people I came across and their backgrounds. I would see people's behaviour, either eating at the dry mess, then watching socially, drinking at the wet mess or at the local alcohol facilities at the camp site. I witnessed the behaviour of people at times that was showing they were in chaos, frustrated, angry, and using aggressive language that I believe was not acceptable on a mine site, or any workplace in fact. But others would tell you otherwise. I could see incredible pressure on people's faces starting to surface and their behaviours were worrying. In a lot of cases, young men and women I did see looked like they were feeling all sorts of health un-wellness, and possible early signs of depression and anxiety.

This experience of living on a mine site is another life in itself. The life of a FIFO worker can either begin at the start of the day when the alarm goes off, or at the other end of the day when the sun is about to go down. Now this is nothing new, mining in Australia has been around for hundreds of years, likewise in other parts of the world. I found there were some key areas to how this professional life of work may impact on us. There are some identified areas such as our nutritional or food intakes, to getting enough sleep, the necessary activity after work, monitoring our hygiene levels, behaviour affecting operations, taking care of our clothes and maintaining some form of grooming. Limiting alcohol and recreational drug intakes that may be accessible on site, bad behaviour, and in some cases the language use, was followed up by aggressive and threatening remarks.

I remember on one occasion I was working at a well-known mining site on the border of WA and South Australia for a couple of weeks. I went to use the clothes washing machine and dryer. A staff member informed me, 'You best stay near your washing machine and dryer, someone will come along and pull them out if all the machines are busy and put their dirty clothes in and leave yours on the ground'. Many times I walked into the washing and dryers hut to see scattered clothes, whether it be wet or dry, on the ground. I also saw poor relationships where people would even up their disagreement with someone on site with physical confrontations.

Fortunately, most mine sites have strong policies to this behaviour and make decisions to remove people from the sites, by terminating or standing someone down until a decision can be determined. With that in mind, theses extra challenges and practices people face in the workplace just adds up again to their health outcomes.

In addition to the lifestyle of a FIFO person is their nutritional dietary intake and the consumption of alcohol. Many times, I saw people beginning a new shift that showed they were just getting over the alcohol from the night before. In some cases, they had little to eat which didn't allow their alcohol to be absorbed overnight. The nutritional level on a mine site was full of fresh fruits, vegies, mixed breads, processed and fatty foods that all looked inviting, and you could have as much as you like. Whether it was breakfast, lunch, or tea. It was like a banquet of food that invited you and yes, FIFO people work long hours and they need to have the energy to perform at work. But in my case, I was over - doing it too and I paid dearly for it down the track.

I will admit myself that I did get carried away with the food that was on offer when I was visiting these sites. I was no saint there, I can tell you. I would also be enticed to grab an extra container of small cupped ice cream to take back to my room, watch a bit of TV and then go to sleep (or take cheese biscuits or cream cakes for desert). I did see my weight balloon out at one stage and I had to haul it back in, take steps to my weight and health in a positive direction, get back to eating the right foods, and maintaining discipline. I was becoming very sluggish, tired, less active, and starting to become a little lazy. I had to change my behaviour quickly. I was looking around me and seeing people who were in good shape when they arrived on site and then noticed that they were deteriorating as quickly as I was.

The increase of poor nutritional foods, less activity or exercise, poor sleeping habits, and high sugar intakes in our drinks only increase the rate of obesity to our bodies. It also increases the risks to further health compilations and then starts the illnesses we did not see coming. Working away on jobs in remote areas further increase our risks, it doesn't matter what age we are as we are all susceptible to letting our health go downhill at a rapid rate. It just furthers the risks of heart disease, obesity, diabetes, and lack of sleep, which all can be the early signs of mental illness. All of these diseases are everywhere in our community, so a proactive approach to people working away would only improve and bring great wealth to our workplace when we are away from home.

Giving that FIFO employment is about working away from home, it takes a lot of discipline to have a balanced life style. In reflection of how our community in general is becoming more an obese society, our workplace can contribute to that if we do not take charge of our health and manage it to ensure we do have a great and enjoyable life. This is not just one of the isolated areas in which people have difficulties adjusting to work and life style balances. We are seeing other shift working professions such as the Police Service, Prisons or Correctional Services, Security Industry, Nursing, Media Outlets, Hotel and Recreational, just to name a few, that have all had their challenges in health and wellness in the past. I know from those industries there have been studies and research to look at how they can improve and educate those workforces to take care of themselves, and into the future of their employment. The impact of our health and surrounding or peripheral life issues only furthers the impact with stress, financial burdens, and other related personal responsibilities.

The increase in our workforce with more generations in employment has been a slow talking point. As I mentioned briefly in an earlier chapter, we are now seeing many generations in the workforce, more so than ever. With the increase of the publicised obesity in our community, where does that fit? Each year a few health reports are presented by our health providers in Australia, by Medibank, HBF and BUPA, who give yearly reports to their own data collection from the services their members use, what is affecting their health and how that will shift into areas such as the workplace. One of the alarming issues was the increase of obesity in our younger generations, in comparison to what it was like in the 1970's. It was shown that in the 1970's, youths aged between five to 16 years old were at eleven percent overweight, and that same age group now in 2018 is 28 percent.

We have gone from an overweight society to an obese society in forty years; we have gone threefold. With that in mind, what does our future workforce look like in ten, twenty or thirty years from now? That is an alarming problem for both employees and businesses. How will it affect you in due time? What costs will be associated to your business or an employee and what threat is it to your quality of life and your family? We are now in trouble times with our health in the workplace.

My purpose for this book is to encourage people to consider their health as being paramount to their living. You may have the best education, the best job, be paid well for doing your work, but if you are not well, living with a chronic disease that was preventable and is affecting your day to work performance, then are you going well? You have time to address it or improve your health status, we all do. If we were to take a stand, we can start to minimise those other illnesses and cancers along with mental illness challenges.

The risks with an obese workforce are such that we bring other illnesses into the equation such as Depression, Bipolar, Multiple Sclerosis, Dementia, and Post Traumatic Syndrome Disorder just to name a few. We have seen in recent years an increase in people in the workplace being confronted with the above diagnosis. Medication levels have increased, moods have shifted and changed, and the ability to recall and articulate made difficult with work duties, are ever so clear when being at the front desk at work. The experiencing of low self-esteem, feeling guilty of not performing at work, having great difficulties getting up out of bed each day for work and behaviours that just indicate isolation from people becomes very bleak. The outcomes are so impactful on people they lose their identity, lose their family, relationships, and in some cases, this leads to a not-so-happy conclusion.

The workplace is a place where people can reclaim their life. We are seeing or hearing of increases in suicides in our community, and while it is mostly young males, they are either self-inflicting, suiciding, or causing injuries to themselves. Young women are experiencing more anxiety and depressive disorders. This puts added risks for our workplace and employers. It is most difficult to determine how anyone will handle working a job, in the beginning it can an exciting time, the opportunity to earn a good income, accommodation and food provided, it all appears laid on. But after a while the other peripherals of our life start to surface, and pressure and stress mounts, and then we see incidents that are unexplainable when they occur. The FIFO on any mine site have now taken great care to having support staff and services to aid those in troubled times. We now have external services that were initiated by ex FIFO workers to support those in need of counselling and support. Living away from home is not for the faint hearted, there is more to the life of a FIFO worker, and it's most important that we are engaging in all forms of the operation to ensure we reduce any possible threat and harm to each other. Our health and emotional and mental state of mind will be tested, and that's when we need to put our hand up and ask for help.

In the next chapter I will endeavour to break down our life patterns with our professions and see what we do and how we do it. It can give us an understanding and then we can leave the self-judgment behind and cut ourselves some slack.

We spend the best part of our life at work to build the great Australian dream for ourselves, for our loved ones and family, and yet we are putting our future happiness on the line. Life goes quickly, and, in some cases, we do not know when it will end at all. I see people living a life of a facade, feeling they are bullet proof with the attitude 'It won't happen to me', when the truth is, we are not well in our community. Now is the time to reconsider ourselves and take care of our health so that we can enjoy life with vitality and plenty of activity, whether we are at home or at work.

It is so important that we support and inspire our existing future generations as they will be carrying on the baton at some stage, and they have our legacy to ensure they enjoy life pain free, and with a working life that gives them great hope and success. To lose a generation or two through poor life style would be an injustice to them, in the end we did bring them into this world and they did not have a say in the matter. At least we could ensure that they are well and become even wiser to their own future health that is passed onto other and future generations. I would encourage my son to do that, to encourage his future kids and grandkids, that taking care of yourself is paramount to an enjoyable life.

With the work I deliver in the Human Behaviour Excellence programs, along with experts in their fields, the focus is of making our workplace safe and inspiring, with future health and wellness in mind. Our primary focus is always to bring awareness, to inform and deliver programs that will make a difference to the health and behaviour of the workplace, and to encourage businesses to enjoy the involvement with their staff to providing a place of great connection and success. Nothing is more gratifying than to be affecting people and their self-growth towards health and future personal success with a fresh, new, behavioural outlook.

'But underneath it all, people are having a huge challenge with working with their health'

Reclaiming Your Working Life

Almost ninety percent of our workforce, during their working life, will work indoors. It is amazing that we enclose ourselves throughout working life in confined and close environments, and at the end of the day, are they serving our health positively? In this chapter I would like to discuss the areas of our working life that I feel are impacting on our balance of life, health, and relationships in all forms, and what that may be doing to us emotionally and physically.

During our working life, we may experience shifts and changes to our hours of work or it may be that you are employed at the one place all your life. The latter is rare; these days not many people stay in the same job for their entire life time. If you look back to earlier years of the labour force and one example of that would be the Ford Motor Car Company, started by Henry Ford in the 1890's, employed people on production lines for eight hours a day and five days a week. His systematic approach to employing, and his production line approach, became the culture for the next 100 or so years and is still done to this day in the car industry. Our approach to the workforce has change dramatically and in fact it has been turned upside down. In future generations, people are going to change jobs or pathways about 20 or 30 times in their working life.

Our whole working hours have seen changes, from our starting to finishing times of the day. As mentioned earlier, we are seeing more part-time work, casual hours, and contracting, to name a few examples of the changes to how people are doing their work. Not knowing when you will work or what hours you will work can be stressful, let alone your personal circumstances for example financial, raising the family, or staying in touch socially.

What is clear and is further taking charge of our lives, is that more people are working away from their homes than they once did. For example in Perth, Western Australia, when I first arrived here from Sydney in 1982 to take up work, the Perth Metropolitan area was seen to be thirty minutes outside the Perth Central Business District. Now in 2018, we are seeing people live an hour to an hour and a half away. The Perth Metropolitan, like other areas, has grown and spread out over the past 30 or so years I have been here. The urban sprawl, the increase in our highways, transport infrastructures, and the rapid rise in shopping centres being built, has seen people move to those areas and establish homes to raise their families. There are many reasons as to why Perth has evolved over that period. What does that do to our working life both emotionally and physically, or to our balance of lifestyle? This urbanisation is not only restricted to Perth, but all towns and cities throughout Australia.

If we look at our current working life, in most cases, people are continuing to drive for lengthy periods of time or catching a train that could take anywhere between an hour to ninety minutes depending on where you live or more. A good example is the Blue Mountains train lines in New South Wales, where people travel approximately two hours to and from work. There are other forms of transport like cycling, where cyclists are able use cycle ways to ride to work, and that varies due to the distances they live, once again, from home to work. What is interesting there is a great focus by governments in Australia to ensure there are adequate cycle ways throughout the metropolitan areas in the respective cities of Australia. Great for physical health and wellbeing, encouraging people to be active and maintain a good balance of exercise. Cycle and walkways are a great initiative by our governments and town planners, and we should be encouraging everyone to utilise them to keep active and healthy.

Let us go to the experience of our day to day life of sitting in a car and driving to and from work. What future health risks are we potentially going to experience? But before we go there, did you get enough sleep last night? Did you have a broken sleep, are your sleeping patterns way wards, do you get much sleep at all historically, how long have you been having difficulties sleeping and getting the rest you need? Throughout my life I have spoken to countless people about their inability to get their desired amount of rest and sleep. I know of people who just barely get three hours of sleep per night. What is that doing to our health, our ability to function and focus on work, let alone having to pull the car out of the driveway and head into work for an hour's drive? I know in some circumstances couples have a newly born child and that throws all sorts of obstacles into play, when the child needs to be fed throughout the night and this causes broken sleep and tiredness and fatigue, until the young child can sleep through the night. There are many reasons why people are losing sleep or not getting consistent rest and it will affect our health and our ability to heal if we are confronted with an illness, a trauma, or a virus.

In reflection, going back some decades in Australia, we didn't have the culture of a siesta as opposed to it being part of the culture in other countries. Whereby people go home for an hour or two, have a short sleep then come back to work and feel totally relaxed and energised. I recall, as a young person living in my home town of Halls Creek, Western Australia in the very late sixties and early seventies, my parents and the town would shut down for a couple of hours of the day after 12 midday and then return to work at 2pm. Looking back, I guess I can now see the advantages, and mind you, the lifestyle was different back then, there was no TV, Internet, and no modified communications systems. Only ABC Radio when transmission was able to get through to bring the world closer together. Working life has changed since those days and everyone now is accessible twenty-four-seven, or we have allowed that to take place, in fact. I wonder now, looking back at the benefits to my parents having siestas in the middle of the day back then. I am sure they were able to reduce their stresses, rest up, catch up on sleep and feel revitalised and alert for the afternoon at work.

I can recall a personal experience some years ago, I was having great difficulty in sleeping through the night, broken sleep, loss of breath, heavy snoring, feeling fatigue at work, dozing off in the afternoons in meetings and work hours in the office. It was affecting me. I was not exercising, I was thirty or forty kilos over weight, I could barely tie up my shoe laces and when I did I was out of breath.

Some years prior to this experience I was fit, kept in good physical presence, I was actively umpiring football in the winter, playing cricket in the summer and every month taking part in the local triathlons competitions in Perth. Due to my work shifts with working on the mines sites as mentioned in the last chapter, my health was beginning to suffer and not only that, but it showed as well. I had people telling me to look after myself, get a check-up and to get back out into life. I took a call one day from my Uncle Peter Bridge, he said he was concerned for my health and really just sending me encouragement. I will never forget that call, he was calling because he cared for me, it was one of those calls that just had to inspire you to get on and get healthy again. I did have a light bulb experience around that time apart from the call I had from Peter, but I may share that at another time. My weight ballooned due to poor eating habits and no exercise and feeling tired in between and not energised to do anything. But in the meantime I was not really resting, my lifestyle was erratic with working away and keeping a relationship and reducing the stresses of both was challenging for me. Since that day, which is almost eight years ago, I set about rejuvenating my health and activity. Now I am back umpiring, playing cricket, running regular Perth fun runs and included a couple of half marathons.

But let me tell you the worth of investment in myself of when I was losing my weight and how that impacted on me and the outcomes I received from that. When I started out to lose my excessive weight, I looked at some basic steps, not fancy approaches, just simple things I could do. I would walk each day, get out, be active in the fresh air, get some sunlight, fresh oxygen, drink plenty of water, and cut down on the processed foods, sugar and salts. I went cold turkey with my eating and drinking. I will say I don't drink alcohol and have not socially for many years, but I was drinking a bit of soft drink, fruit juices and flavoured milks and I knew that all had to go.

So, I set about getting my health back on track and over the next six to twelve months I was able to reduce my weight by twenty kilos. Through having stir fry each night, the odd cup of tea, natural yoghurt, and a walk each night that went from thirty minutes to an hour to two per night. It was when I lost the twenty or so kilos, I set about seeing if I could jog a little again, and little by little I did more and more, and then trimmed my weight down further.

Within twelve months I was back running in the Perth's City to Surf 12 Kilometre Fun Run in 2010. Fortunately, I have a great friend and running mate in Robert MacFarland he gave me great support and encouragement. We would run each week leading up to our events. We ended up running two half Marathons together. Thanks Robbie Mac you're a legend. But during that period of trimming the weight off, eating well and exercising, things took a positive change. I could sleep through the night, my snoring had stopped, I was not losing my breath, my overall activity and energy was improving all the time, and I could tie up my shoes laces without getting out of breath. One reason as to why I feel my sleeping patterns improved and snoring was reduced, was I believe through reducing fatty tissues around my neck that was pressing and restricting my airways. These days I don't suffer with snoring or breathlessness, and at times I may have a broken sleep but more often than not, I sleep well. I put my sleeping improvements down to a change of nutrition, exercise, and losing weight to improve my sleep patterns and get rid of my snoring habit.

From a personal experience and back to the original question I asked you, did you get enough sleep last night? Well did you, and if you didn't, how that will affect you going to work today? It is so important to your functioning in life, we must encourage ourselves to investigate how to get enough rest and sleep. I knew from a personal sense I had to take responsibility for that and no one else but me. I had to take charge of my health. I was running my body and I was accountable, and I was intent to ensure I was not going to die at around fifty years of age due to poor health, and not have the ability to run and play sport with my son Jarod. There were other factors to me improving my lifestyle but changing my focus on my health and activity was what I needed to do and to be sure I could at least function in my day to day of life.

So I have given you an insight to my thoughts on sleeping. I guess I was fortunate I was not needing to attend a medical specialist and be diagnosed with sleep apnoea, with which I have close family members struggling with that issue. So, take care of yourself, get plenty of rest and enjoy getting out there.

Now, what about our drive into work today and how has that impacted on you and your wellness to get through the day? As mentioned earlier in this chapter our travel times to work have increased in the past thirty or so years, especially in the Perth area. We are seeing people leave for work earlier and earlier nowadays to beat the peak hours of traffic, bumper to bumper, congestion of cars on the increase, our concentration needed to be at an optimum level, stress levels increase with our manoeuvring of vehicles and the lists goes on. When sitting in your car, how are you feeling? Are you feeling tired and worn out before getting into your car, feeling fatigued, and feeling stressed for the job you have? Are you enjoying your workplace? Did you look forward to getting up out of bed to go to work? I am sure some of these I have experienced over the many years of my working life. To sit in traffic and consciously watch front, left, right and rear, takes its toll on everyone and at some stage, something will break, and you become unwell and begin to take on illnesses which you never had experienced before.

With everything on our mind, the hidden issues of family, finances, children to be taken care of, loved ones not well, we are stressed or experiencing health issues ourselves and on forms of medication to help us to get through the day. Life is challenging at times, both emotionally and physically. Now that you have finally arrived at work, you are driving around for a car park and in your case, it may be that you have to use paid parking. You drive up the ramps, around and around you go to the top level of the carpark building and get the final spot. Phew, you say to yourself, I am here, now I must get motivated for my day of work. Look back on your journey into work, what sorts of stress and thoughts went through your head at the very start of your day? I see people really doing it tough coming to work, it's as if we are on auto pilot, we are programmed by habit and yet we are all dealing with something and now we are about to step into our workplace, show a presence and be ready for the day ahead.

What goes on in your mind coming into work, are you ready to tackle the KPIs of the day, is your workplace filled with great joy or is there toxicity? Are your work colleagues approachable and caring? What's your management systems like and management towards you in their supervision of your work and workload? There is a tremendous amount of internal feelings and thoughts that go through our heads day to day, and if your workplace is not enjoyable and you are stressed from the onset, it becomes a long day at the office and it becomes stressful and resentful too. If you and your workplace environment are not aligned with each other, you will have difficulties with your performance and getting some self-satisfaction and enjoyment.

Our ability to function at work positively and productively is always going to be a reflection of our personal issues, whether they be at work or outside of this. It is easy for people to say, "Leave it at the front door", but at the time, we can't. How do we mange that? We are creatures of habit by nature, and so we need to identify what's appropriate to bring into the workplace and what's not. Being able to visit your workplace manager or HR person could be the first step to getting clarity, or there may be support systems in place or counsellors on site to assist you, or the company may source relevant expertise.

Managing your workplace life is not easy when you enter working environments with other people, and the demands that business put on their staff to perform and reach targets has never changed. Depending on how we are feeling, our private lives, financial commitments and health, our focus to work will have a significant effect on the outcome at the end. One of the things I learnt during my time studying naturopathy was the conscious thoughts to my day to day work. More so, the way I was functioning with eating habits, drinking, getting plenty of air, getting sunlight, having short breaks, and really investing in my lunch time breaks. For us to have long term careers or open opportunities for further work, we need to have a balanced approach. That reduces the stresses and the potential to minimise the early onset of chronic illness or other personal reactions such as depression or initial stages of mental health issues.

As I mentioned in the beginning of this chapter, most people will work indoors for nearly ninety percent of their working life. How does that affect us and what are the short and long-term challenges with that?

The chance to reorganise your day of work and utilising the breaks you have in the workplace is there for you to consider. We should be encouraging people to get out at lunch time and get walking, to eat out in the fresh air instead of in the office lunch room. A lot of times we are just as keen to go to the lunch room, make a cup of tea or coffee and sit down with our lunch, and enjoy the thirty or so minutes we have before getting back to it. The opportunity to get outside to walk a bit and have a snack in the fresh air is so positive for you and your body, and for your stress as well. We should be also encouraging people in the workplace to drink more water, we dehydrate, and regular water intake revitalises our body, settles our systems down and keeps our body at a regulated temperature that allows us to function and concentrate as well. I will talk about the importance of regular water intake in a later chapter with a personal experience I had, and how relevant it was when I was in the workplace at that time. The advantages to walking and if possible, rigorous running exercises in your breaks during the day at work as well. It just allows you to reduce those stresses and keeps us vibrant with our work and helps with concentration.

In summary to this chapter, I have only just scratched the surface, but I hope I have you thinking and that you begin to look at where you can be inspired to have a good future life, not just in your private life, but in the workforce where you will spend a great deal of your time. Our ability to reclaim our workplace control and how we respond is in our hands. As mentioned in an earlier chapter our workforce has changed and the opportunity to reinvent ourselves both from a skills-based sense and health development for a long-term employment progress is in our hands. We are now at that stage to finally decide for ourselves and for businesses to recognise they too have a responsibility, to be active and embrace a new way of meeting their employee's needs, as well as the business needs, for a win-win situation. A new form of leadership that is very inclusive of health in mind will only increase goodwill between employee and employer.

We must consider our wellbeing into the future. It will be a tough and long road, but the chance to have a vibrant life, filled with activity, fun and enjoyment, and be able to share that with loved ones and friends and work associates, is there for us to take. Wouldn't it be a great example of human spirit to see that people can approach their employer to say that something's not right, and not be judged, but to be considered sensitively and respectfully? When we achieve that scenario of positive behaviour, responses and attitudes rise, and we then minimise the stress and pain that adds to our existing or future health problems in the workplace. Then our future generations will reap the benefits of our legacy and they will be entrusted to take the baton and lead the way. It is worth progressing towards.

'If you and your workplace environment are not aligned with each other, then you'll have difficulties with your performance and above all, getting some self-satisfaction and enjoyment.'

The Impact of Peripheral Factors

As you have read so far, I have at times referenced that our chronic illnesses are further compounded with work related stress and an unbalanced lifestyle. We discussed in Chapter 5 the opportunity to reclaim ourselves back to looking at where we can improve our lives. This chapter is an overview of some of the other personal problems we may face while working through our compounding health problems. There is so much of our lives taken up with non-productive and time wasting processes, that it creates a reactive response in our behaviour both physically and emotionally.

Invariably, if not dealt with we end up stressed, fatigued or experiencing forms of depression and anxieties. The peripheral factors are those that bring out the best and worst in us and if not harnessed or worked through, will cause us to take a shift for the worse. Not only for our health, but our ability to function in the workplace is critical to our existence to give and perform good, self-satisfying and productive work.

Many of us right now are working through family and relationship issues, let alone our work pressures. It's like a coin tossed in the air, landing on either heads or tails. 'Luck of the draw they say'. There are many variables to relationships and the dynamics are far and wide as to how your scenario will pan out. When couples decide to part, all the mixed emotions and behaviours come to the surface and we start to see the real personalities in play. The influences of a breakdown in a relationship or marriage is a very hurtful, resentful, angry, blame game, loss of love, loss of connection experience. Then you involve children in the separation and that takes on a whole new ball game. Who gets the kids? Can the parties amicably work through it to ensure everyone is able to communicate and behave as an adult?

The first stages of separation once again put further stress and strain on individuals. Health starts to decline, people withdraw from contact with others, feeling sorry for themselves… at the end of the day, what do we do to get our life back on track? This can be a complicated process to do and start with. With so many thoughts and stresses going on it can be most difficult to come to some reason and clarity.

Going through a separation, moving out of home and letting loved ones and respected work colleagues know there are new life arrangements, can all be most stressful and without the emotion of 'why' it all came to this. With separation brings arrangements of how you will manage seeing the children. Who gets custody or shared custody, and in a lot of cases, battle for custody takes place? Many mixed emotions and the temptation for physical confrontations with other parties can arise in the early stages of relationships breaking up. When we include child maintenance and custody to seeing children, all new dynamics take place. In many cases there is no win – win here and the children end up being the pawn on the table with parents unable to compromise or work through the old fear, ego and control. Everyone becomes angry, hostile, aggressive, and the blame game takes on a new dimension. Nobody goes anywhere except to the Court House.

I have seen examples in my time where separating couples did come to the table and amicably work through it, even though it was like walking on egg shells initially. They did it and great relationships came from it. Separation in relationships are not easy and in fact they are gut wrenching and heartbreaking experiences. I have experienced this on a couple of occasions, it's a surreal experience, but its life, and we must work our way to leaving relationships with some positivity. If we do not manage the break up, our other passions and interests in life will be tucked away in the corner never to return, and then we continue down a road of low self-esteem and our health will be affected.

Now that it is out in the open, separation taken place, there are children and their wellbeing to focus on. Your family influences may be positive or negative, with advice, financial challenges, and the dividing of assets. You may be in business yourself and with that you will need to seek an expert in law to advise you. But all along you need to watch your health, be wise to what is affecting you emotionally and physically. You may wish to visit a counsellor or a professional in the field of personal management to ensure you are ok and able to rationalise what has taken place. It is a most stressful and strained time, and it is easy to be caught up in the emotions of it all. At the end of the day, you have one life and somehow you need to be encouraged to take a step back and take a deep breath and work through it.

In the times when I was challenged with this experience, I just felt I needed to sit back and be quiet, regather myself, knowing a decision was made and now, how do we move forward from here. And while the other party need to be aligned with you, they too are going through their own processes or emotions and they are dealing with it the best they can. It is so important for everyone to work through this in an adult way and reduce the power play games and controlling behaviours that draw the worst out of us. There are no winners in this, it only increases the anger and continues to rip the guts out of people for each other. In most cases the children feel the brunt of all this, and they too become ill and lose their confidence to life. They also take on the stress, feel the loss, withdraw, and in a lot of cases, children's welfare is not taken into consideration from parents and close ones. Their whole home environment has been turned over and they start to feel un-wellness and they go to school not wanting to be there. But in some ways school may be a great place for them to look forward to going as it gets them away from the disruption at home.

Having now discussed relationships briefly in terms of separation, what may be the direction it will take in the future? There are other stresses and strains that impact on intimate relationships, not just possible break ups or finances. It's also the intimate connection between you and your partner. In cases we have seen where people, due to their workload and busy commitments, have lost their intimacy for each other. I guess the question I ask is, what was the reason you came together in the first?

I have observed in my life, that when people are happy together they are in good health and wellness. I know we only see the exteriors of people's lives, but when you really see couples enjoying each other's company and working in congruency together they appear in great spirits with one another. This has a flow on affect to other parts of our lives and more so in our working life, as when couples join to harness their relationship, they then bring other people along and their children to embrace harmony in their environment. It is no different from the workplace, a happy and enjoyable home environment will lead to developing great relationships and helps immensely to overcoming challenges that are faced in the future. One of these challenges is possibly one of the parties falling ill and then the family unit click in and provide the support and love to get through it.

I want to share with you an experience I had personally in a relationship and I felt my health status then was a great part of the problem. I also felt in my mind it could affect my continual relationship. I was having great difficulty having intimacy with my partner. I became incredibly unaroused, and never in my life had I experienced this. Physiologically I was absolutely dismayed at how I could get to this stage of my life and not be able to enjoy the pleasures, and for my partner to also experience the pleasure of two people embracing one another. I had a number of things run through my mind, I was seeing what other factors were going on in my life. I looked at what I was eating, what could affect my sexual drive. I wasn't drinking enough water and I wasn't taking any alcohol. I don't smoke. There were indications that I was not getting the rest and sleep I normally did. Looking back there was fatigue, as I was dozing off in the afternoon at work trying to keep my eyes open. But physiologically, I was dumfounded to this current experience. I felt I lacked as a person, I was experiencing a form of low self-esteem, and my stress levels were increasing.

I wanted to enjoy my sexual experiences with my partner and I could not. Fortunately, my partner was so understanding and at no any point did she cast judgement on me. She was frustrated, I know, but never dropped her support towards me. I will admit I spoke to close male friends about my situation and they too themselves had similar experiences in their past. They recommended me to see my GP and be asked to be prescribed Viagra. Not one for being on or taking prescribed medication, I thought, well is there something more going on that I am doing with my body and health that is preventing me from enjoying my sexual pleasures? I then considered my mild fatigue experiences, my issues of not getting enough rest or broken sleep patterns at the time, drinking a fair bit of coffee, good nutritional balance but an increase in my starchy processed foods, my steady weight gain and lack of water intake. If I was drinking water it was less than a litre per day.

After analysing it, my recent outcomes, and the possibilities of what may be also impacting on my sexual pleasure and having an honest look at my habits, I decided to make changes with my nutritional intake, my exercise, reducing caffeine and drinking plenty of water. I felt it was one of the biggest concerns for me, that I was not drinking enough water and that I was very dehydrated. I could tell by my urine that I was dehydrated. I did experience light headedness at times, and whenever I have been down this road of feeling light headed, it was due to a lack of water.

I then cast back to my place of work at the time, I was sitting upstairs with the sun bearing down on me each day, not drinking water, and I believe I was experiencing dehydration that had much to do with my erectile dysfunction. When I started to address these areas, I was on my journey back to positive health again. I had never considered that dehydration could be an influence on my erectile dysfunction. This is only my experience, so always seek professional advice. But also, keep an open mind and be conscious to what you are doing and experiencing, to guide you to a conclusion.

Since then I have had discussions with many men and explained my experience to them. Many men right now are suffering or going through erectile dysfunction and other health issues, both physically and emotionally. As well as women, who are having frustrations with enjoying their sexual relationships and an increase in Urinary Tract Infections, which is causing discomfort and anxiety. Both men and women go to work each day with many types of health issues, some are quite easy to talk about, but others are not. This only amplifies the risk of people not talking about their health issues or suffering in silence, and doing it tough as they go through their day to day work. In some cases, if our health is not addressed or improved, our behaviour will come to the surface and there lies another issue. In the next chapter I will discuss more on our behaviour and the effects in the workplace.

Another sensitive area where couples experience stress and financial stress and anxiety, is through In

Vitro Fertilisation or better known as IVF. It has been almost forty years since the first IVF child was born in Australia. It has been a wonderful and embracing moment in people's lives. In some cases, not so positive where couples have not been so successful in IVF outcomes. I have seen couples go through IVF that had not been able to not just conceive and have children, but to have their own children, naturally. I have seen couples not have any success with IVF, and have on several occasions come to a financial crisis and unable to progress forwards without having any children. I have seen couples that did not have success with IVF suddenly separated in their relationships to go their own ways, then to find out down the road those couples that did separate had children to new partners.

The reason I raise this is to let you know I am also the father of an IVF son. He was born in 1999 at the Concept Clinic at King Edward Memorial Hospital in Perth Western Australia. His mum and I were introduced to IVF in the mid-1990s, as both she and I had been trying for a few years prior without any success. It's not until looking back on my path that I have come to realise that there is more to it than the steps both my son's mum and I went through. The challenges couples face in enhancing their family unit, through difficulties in conceiving and with added lifestyle, professional work stress, financial stress, and the increased pressure from surrounding friends and family with the expectation of having children and having them by a certain age, only increases the pressure to be the 'norm' in our society to have children, and in the normal way.

I can only speak from my perspective, but there were emotional personal challenges I faced along the way, that at stages I felt I was not capable of or incapable of performing, in bearing a child with my son's mum. The lack of knowledge and understanding for people undergoing IVF and external friends and family always raised comments of interest.

On occasions, I had experienced comments such as, 'are you shooting blanks', 'are you doing it the right way' or 'do you have it in you to produce a child.' On a personal note or from internalising in my mind, these branding moments do start to change us and we question whether it would ever be possible to be a father. We now see that couples are under increased pressure to have children, and we are finding more couples looking to consider IVF, more so than ever before. I can remember on three occasions having to provide sperm samples, one at the local Medical facility locked away in a little room, another at my home (and then having to bring my sperm in a jar within 30 minutes of ejaculation to the Medical clinic) and thirdly directed to a small room secluded away where I was handed a number of pornographic materials and my sperm capture bottle to assist in the process of producing sperm at the Concept Facility Centre, Subiaco, WA. Then both my son's mother and I waited anxiously for the outcomes of testing results to see whether I had enough sperm to aid in fertilising the egg with my son's mother. On two occasions my son's mother and I had unsuccessful attempts at IVF. The self-consciousness and self-value one has when informed that you are unsuccessful is very much an emotional gut wrenching let down, both for you and your partner. I am only speaking as a male, I have not looked at it from a female's perspective, and I will speak more of that at another time as I intend to write an In Vitro Fertilisation book in the future.

Moving forwards, the science and improvements to IVF over the years has been wonderful for our community, with its ability to engage and unite people through acceptance. It's amazing, as I go through my work and the community, how many people open up about struggling to have children, and in turn it places great pressures on couples in their relationships. It's these challenges couples face in wanting to have children and due to health problems, it is further increased with the stress, let alone the financial aspects to it.

I wanted to share this with you, as we are all going through something, the anxiety, the anticipation, along with trying to keep a life balance and then having to perform at work and keep our careers intact. If we are not on top of our health or checking in with how we are feeling or responding to our day to day life, we are in danger of creating risks to our life balance and wellness into the future.

Our ability to go to work each day with personal issues and on top of that, to impact it with our health problems, is most concerning. Over the years of my working life, I have met some of the most brilliant and skilled people, both male and female. These are not your everyday, high profile people who enjoy the lime light. They come from many backgrounds, from professions of note with highly credentialed qualifications, to tradesman who are just so gifted at their work and could solve the problems of the world if taken seriously, to people who were just able to put their hand to anything at any time and showed a high class of work. There are people that didn't have the best education and who may have left school early to follow their dreams and are creative geniuses, who ended up being great entrepreneurs in our community.

I have only discussed a couple of the areas of peripheral challenges people go through, and if in some form, un-wellness starts to eat at their ability to show their immense potential and talent at the workplace, it is most sad to see. Our workplace in some cases can be our domain or our sanctuary from all the other things in life.

I hope that you can stop for a moment and take a breath and look back upon your journey in the workplace, and acknowledge all the great contributions you have made along the way. That you also acknowledge yourself, and that if you are struggling with your health in some form, you take every step to get yourself back and then move on with boundless joy and harmony. Our workplace can be a fantastic way to build our networks, our connections, our self-worth, and relationships. Now's the time to enjoy it so you can reap the rewards of a fulfilled career to the end.

'I have seen examples in my time where separating couples did come to the table and amicably work through it. Even though it was like walking on eggshells, initially they did it and great relationships came from it.'

Behavioural Change in the Workplace

Is there some connection with our health issues that trigger off the way we behave in the heat of the moment? Is it that we still have not addressed our past life experiences? Or going back even further to the unresolved issues of our childhood, for which today you showed anger, bullying, threatening comments to a staff member or displayed a dictatorial approach with your leadership that at the end of the day created more stress, more anxiety and un-wellness in the workplace?

I sure have seen glimpses of these behaviours from past work colleagues in my working life, and they are not the type of environments I enjoy being part of. The way people behave and communicate tells a lot about their past, and how they got here. From my perspective, there is a combination of wellness, behaviour and their perception of the world that is expressed in communications and behavioural responses.

It is this type of environment and behaviour that starts to take hold of people in the workplace. I have seen people affected by the receiving end of poor behaviour that leads to an illness of some sort. Workplace behaviour in the last ten years has been ever so fascinating to me, we have seen an escalating and dramatic rise in incidences that has taken its toll on both employees and employer. What are the gains that both individual and company get out of displaying poor and unacceptable behaviour for their own advantages? I have conducted many training programs in companies, corporates, and small businesses in the art of dynamics of language. The power of our language, the way we use it and the words we say will tell us everything about who we are and how we see ourselves.

We are seeing an increase in people expressing how they feel, and with platforms like social media, the cultures have been established that we have free licence to comment about people and say unsavoury things. It doesn't stop there. Our workplace is a constant target of negativity and a low self-esteem language approach that serves no one. When in the workplace we should be inspiring people to produce their best work and feel safe to be at work, to create a fun and enjoyable experience, rather than to see the pushing and finger pointing at one another. I only have to reflect to when I was a child of five years old being at school centres, where these were the behaviours displayed back then. Amazingly as adults the same behaviours are still around, and as a cancerous spread throughout our workforce, no wonder people are not well, they are stressed and on the verge of depression and anxiety. People in some cases have not grown up or they just feel the world owes them something. There is no excuse for poor behaviour, people should own it and work out how best they can communicate in a different way.

Looking back over my working life I have seen work colleagues berated, and managers say horrible things to staff, just unfair and unwarranted comments. I recall at times in my early years of employment being spoken to brashly and signs of bullying to go with it.

Nowadays we are seeing workplace policies in place to protect people, who just want to come and do their work and then go home. Policies that protect against aggression, injuries, trauma, bullying, and workplace incidents, have all been instigated through high level lawsuit claims and workplace issues. Policies also protect businesses too, at the end of the day, they are the employer and they need protection as well, and they must protect their standing in the business. Work place health and safety to go hand in hand to ensure a workplace is safe for all, that provides opportunities for employees, associates and customers with their services, while looking after their image and reputation. The outcome is that it is a costly exercise. Once an incident or a report is filed, the matter could go on for a period of time to be resolved and it could also end up in court. We are all accountable for our actions.

Just to give you a recent report, the Chamber of Commerce and Industry Western Australia (CCIWA), published their April edition of Business Pulse's 2018, and there was a reported 25% increase of violence and aggression in the workplace over the past five years that was impacting on business and workplace operations. These figures were based on workers compensation claims by Worksafe WA CCIWA. These figures did not include workplace and employees who were not covered, and this also did not include self-employed people and those who chose not to file a claim. CCIWA, said their office department of Employees' Relations Advice Centre, were receiving several calls a week about aggression incidents, seeking termination advice or the process for dealing with a complaint.

This is only a tip of the iceberg. Is our workforce in a state of chaos or are we not as bad as it is made up to be? You be the judge! There have been too many examples of incidents and behaviour in recent times that tell me things are not well in the business world. We are all consumed with building our future, which is the right thing to do, but are we building our workplace community to ensure everyone can enjoy the experience of doing a good day's work? I have been to and seen many and varied industries in my time. I have seen these industries display their own culture and behaviours, and they are different I can tell you. I have spoken with supervisors, managers, CEO'S and business owners of the short comings to poor behaviour in the workplace, and in a lot of cases, won't even respond or acknowledge something unacceptable is going on. Yes, we are seeing an increase in poor behaviour that is coming at great costs and to the human spirit. The value we place on each other in the workforce, in some cases, is not a positive one. What is the outcome of increased absenteeism that is costing the businesses in Australia billions of dollars each, with people not being at work, with the behaviour displayed impacting on that figure?

I recall back in 2011, I was asked to investigate a workplace behaviour matter that involved a female and a male staff member. I was contract working for an organisation at that stage who was on the verge of having one of their contracts come to an end. The Acting manager at the time had asked me to investigate the matter. To be up front, I didn't have the necessary skills to investigate. I felt it should have been the HR department's responsibility to investigate, as I was involved only in a training consultants' role with this company. What was interesting was that the Acting manager who had asked me to investigate this issue of harassment between two parties, was also bullying me at the same time. When I said that the HR department needed to be involved he said, "I don't want them involved. I want a third-party investigator". Understanding the business and the company's workplace, it became a little uneasy for me to take this task on. But this Acting manager threatened me to either do the investigation or cut my consultancy work out. I approached the HR Department of this company and mentioned what I was experiencing, just to have the incident on file. The HR manager was in full support of me to lodge a complaint, which I did. Without going into the specifics, that behaviour of threatening and aggression is happening every day of the week in the workplace. This is not the first I had experienced this form of threatening approach in my working life, but it raises the point that there is too much of this behaviour going on. So, what is this doing to our wellness in the workforce?

No wonder we are seeing people struggling to go to work, to get up out of bed, feeling the intensity of not enjoying their work, and business having to deal with staff member's unacceptable and harassing behaviours to other members of the workplace. It puts unnecessary costs and strains on the business with absenteeism, the rise in mild and deep depression, the loss of self-value, and the anxiety of fronting up to a toxic place. Let alone the chronic illnesses or a short-term illness an employee may be currently experiencing, compounded with unsafe workplace behaviours.

Just in the last year in Australia, there have been instances where not only our large and formal corporation's businesses like the Australian Football League (AFL) have had issues of internal bad behaviour but also our most notable services departments have come under notice for their behaviour too. Services included Nursing and administration hospital staff, the Police Services, Corrective Services, our SAS Officer and Army Service, and in our political fields of State and Federal Government, local governments recorded incidences of staff members of poor behaviour. It was interesting I met with a Federal Minister in June 2018 around a table discussion with community people, the Minister asked me what I did and told him I work in the behaviour field and how it was affecting the workforce. His response was of no interest, it was if there was nothing going on in the workplace. There were people sitting either side of me at the time, and one stated that they felt that the way politicians were behaving, as they were entrusted to lead our country, should show some form of professionalism and behave in an adult fashion, and that this was not being demonstrated. No response was given by the Minister, meeting dated and documented by me.

The impacts of unnecessary behaviour take its toll on all areas of the workplace and then flows onto our health. We see employees having time off with stress leave due to sexual harassment, trauma and aggression, with managers and senior managers exerting their presence on individuals. A report by the Mental Health Australia in 2018 had shown that one in five Australians in the workforce in any given year will experience mental health issues. The report did highlight and said there were opportunities for the government and employers to be proactive and look at better support services when in the workplace to help their staff. The mental health crisis is seen to be around $60 billion dollars a year, and if not invested or ways found to improve mental health, the risks for increase and for more community experiencing mental health issues was not going to stop. The report did show that there were significant improvements and breaking down of the stereotypes associated with conditions such as anxiety disorder, depression and post-traumatic stress disorder, the stigma was still alive and well. The worrying signs are there, that it will continue to rise, and the workplace will, in the future, become more unwell.

We know of cases where medication is prescribed, but once non-medication or illicit drugs are used in the workplace we are in dangerous territory. If the correct medication is not prescribed for use while people are in the workplace, what risks and safety are there to all involved? If individuals are experiencing mental health issues and they are in the workforce it does have a range of impacts. It can create an environment of embarrassment, isolation and being misunderstood. What this also does, is it further impacts on the individual employee's career aspirations, that it may possibly get cut short, and then they lose their identity and vitality to get through their mental illness. The support and resources around them will be key to their recovery and to some, hope of feeling their 'normalness' once again. Invariably what we do know is that it can be a slow and progressive road to recovery, and, in some cases, some may never recover. What a shame to have brilliant and talented people in our community unable to show their class in the workforce.

The pressure for employees to have the erratic working hours of part time, casual, on call or long hours, for example FIFO, is causing problems with fatigue. There are cases where employers over load staff with long hours of work, which means more time away from home and a balanced life style. Studies found by the Columbia University, New York, who researched over 8000 workers over 45 years of age, found that hours being varied and long, with inactivity to their roles, will increase their risk of premature death. The researchers said that people sitting in their office for long periods had a similar effect to smoking and this highlights a warning to further health risks in the workplace. Businesses want their employees to increase their productivity and work longer hours but are increasing fatigue and tiredness without negotiating the employee's health. We will see health in the workplace deteriorate even more. Who is to take responsibility for that? Is it an individual or businesses problem or shared responsibility at the end?

In the last couple of years in the business market in Australia, we have seen a downturn in business and people laid off, with changes to how we do business. This has caused business to reassess where they are going and/or whether they stay in the market or move to other areas of business. This has a downward effect, as the employees are then having to adjust their personal lives due to the shift in hours from fulltime to part time, casual hours as such or have their positions made redundant, terminated, or paid out with their entitlements to then go find other work. We must do what we can to ease the uncertainty or manage people better, so we can assist them and to value them in their health progression. The ongoing stress and anxiety is increasing and especially with our younger generation who are more susceptible to suicide, developing anxiety disorders and depression, due to the pressures around them. Yes, our younger generation is facing their own health issues in the future, and their employment prospects of being well and working out their place in the workforce will affect their own quality of life.

So, we are seeing business behaviours change more so than ever, more introductions of the micro business with people looking to create their own industries, or contract to, or consult to, and finding other ways to supplement their incomes and build their opportunities into the future. More businesses are using private labour hire companies, which is not new, but in recent times we have seen new players small and large come into the market. These have all started out from people retrenched or terminated from their fields of expertise, who are now providing contractual labour work. We do also know that people are happy to shift from full time work to part time work to embrace their life style, and what we are seeing is a flexible approach to employment, which means people may choose to do different jobs in their chosen professions or just simply want a change from what they doing, to meet their needs and have some enjoyment. In Western Australia, due to the recent economy over the last couple of years, there has been an upsurge in part time work. People are also not doing the types of work they were performing eighteen months to two years earlier, in a lot of cases, due the shifts and changes in some industries.

Another area of change is the older generation staying in the workforce longer than expected. We are seeing more of the older generations wanting to stay in the workforce, due to possible financial requirements, to keep their hand in, as they feel they still have something to offer and are still enjoy working and going to work. We have seen and heard at times that people over the age of 50 have been over-looked for jobs, promotions, and up-skilling of training on the grounds of their age. This falls in line with the related discrimination that workers may not be enthusiastic or able to adjust quickly in the jobs, or may not be creative enough, so they are passed over for the positions.

There may be the thought that older workers are not fit or healthy to do their work and are more susceptible to injury in the workplace. This causes employers to not risk employing mature aged workers, who still have a great deal to provide in leadership, encouraging team work, who have generated a strong history of contacts and connections, strong communications, and, in most cases, loyalty, reliability and stability. These values are extremely attractive to businesses moving forwards, the older generations may not have the technological wizardry of the other generations, but they will have quality of skills that are most effective in business building and forward progression. The older generation do come with experience and life experience, which can have a positive flow onto the rest of the team.

I have seen many changes taking place in our workforce, there is the uncertainty of its direction into the future, where businesses and people will move with their work. I believe our business and employment opportunities into the future will be ever so exciting. I am looking forward to being in there and taking part for some time yet. How we are all going to respond will be the challenge for each of us.

Our workplace has seen meaningful change in how it does its business, that in staying in the marketplace it needs to operate differently than it once did. While this creates uncertainty and doubt in employees, it also propels individuals to establish their own opportunities, and we are now seeing this take place with more micro businesses. At the end of the day, everyone wants an excellent quality of life for themselves and for their families.

In all of this maze of the workplace and its behaviours, is our health being compromised to ensure we do have a certain quality of life? Are we seeing enough businesses show new forms of leadership to encourage their staff to enjoy a wellness of life and take care of ourselves? Is it within a business or company's interests to encourage their staff to stay well, when at the end of the day, businesses do employ people, and possibly for long periods of time?

What cost for the employer to NOT invest in their staff, with training in health and wellness and behavioural programs that minimise the risks all round in the future? When in the distance looms worker's compensation claims, litigation, workplace issues that will see high payout costs for unfair dismissals, aggression, trauma, or harassment claims in the workplace? Is it a lack of foresight or is it the employer's responsibility to take the lead?

On the other hand, does the employee need to look at their health issues more closely, to improve their ability to function well in the community before going to work? Does the individual need to be responsible for their own health, or more so, to be more conscious of it instead of just letting it pass and in the end, let it catch us out? With more information than ever before at our fingertips, and the advancement in medical science and alternative approaches to our health, it's now a wonderful time for people to review their health status and begin to take hold of it, before it takes hold of them.

We are now approaching some most exciting and innovative times in the workplace, and it would be a shame to not be part of it and enjoy great moments of fulfilment while working. We must also encourage our younger generations to embrace their health as they are looked upon to take us, and their children and businesses, into the future. Their wellbeing will be crucial as they are starting to experience health issues on the rise with anxiety disorders, depression, increased stress and asthma issues, with high reports of increase in the current 16 -24 year age group in our community. We all need to take the lead and see how we can improve and encourage all those around us to enjoy their work and a better quality of life. Our behaviour needs to be investigated and ways to be found for the workplace to make it an environment worth coming to. Through health will be the first steps to having a long and abundant life in the workplace.

'We are all consumed with building our future, which is the right thing to do, but are we building our workplace community to ensure everyone can enjoy the experience in doing a good day's work.'

Where are we Headed?

It is very clear that our workplace and the environments that we work in will change into the future. We have only to look back on our own journeys to see what it did look like, and how it looks today. The demands for people to work longer hours, more jobs and employment conditions that need part time, casual and shared hours to suit the business world, or even the employees. Since the end of World War II, our workplace has increased with generations, and we are almost 6 generations in, serving with values, purpose, and hopefully, with positive intent to leave a legacy for future generations.

The explosion of the generations in the workforce has come at a rapid rate. I started to take notice of it in 2008, while I was consulting for a large corporation and noticed the age groups and the length of years from the youngest to the oldest. A fitting example would be if you go into your local supermarket. You have people of the age of mid to late sixties, to a young person of thirteen or fourteen years of age still at high school. You will see staff of all ages doing a range of tasks but feeling inclusive in the workplace. There are tremendous advantages to having a wide diverse of generations in the workplace. It gives you a blend of savvy techno youths with their ability to adapt, understand technology and have a great connection within their groups with social media. They too are keen to work with the older workforce, and it appears they do have fun and enjoyment. The older workforce come with experience, stability and reliability, which are the values that most businesses see as the key to them staying in the market place, and keeping a high profile or reputation intact. So, with this blend of generations in the workplace, it only lends a positive progression for the decades to come.

Not only has our workforce changed with the inclusion of more generations, we have also seen a change in the way businesses operates. We are seeing more businesses looking to either diversify their business opportunities, change their products, restructure their product base, implement more robotic lines of machinery to reduce staff, or make their business more efficient. We have seen for example, the inclusions in the mining sector with their large and heavy machinery working onsite, with drivers sitting in a control room thousands of kilometres away.

There are more automative services now, we only have to call to pay our electricity or telephone account and speak to what we think is a person on the end of the line that will ask us questions and we then follow the steps to finalising our accounts without ever speaking to someone. This is only the tip of the iceberg, we have only to sit back for a moment and realise the change and what we have experienced along the way. It looks like to me that we are in the age of reinventing ourselves, businesses and employees are in constant change and your future will be challenged, because the jobs you are doing today may not be around tomorrow, next week, next year or in five years' time.

As mentioned in an earlier chapter, micro businesses and more entrepreneurial based businesses are exploding like we have not seen before, and this tells me that businesses will change, and people are now looking at their futures more in-depth than they once did. Our current workplace is still producing traditional work as having been done in previous years, but whether that takes on a new shape in the future will no doubt be governed by our marketplace, our services and the need for services, or we may possibly see those roles go and never return.

Job uncertainty is impacting on the current workplace and with the added peaks and troughs of the mining and construction industries in recent times in Australia, likely the end of the mining boom in Western Australia, workers are looking to perform alternative jobs and further up-skilling to stay ahead of the changes in the future. Another increase we are seeing is the awareness of individuals coming into the workforce or re-entering the workplace having to up-skill themselves to have that x factor in getting a position. The changing of the job market is also seeing an increase in up-skilling, either through re-attending school to complete year 12 High School Certificates, taking on University studies, or visiting Registered Training organisations to acquire relevant training and a skills base to pursue new career pathway changes. With our workforce, our jobs, our businesses under ever increasing change and uncertainty, everyone is now having to be proactive towards their work in the future. As mentioned in an earlier chapter, young generations coming into the workforce could have anything up to 20 or so job changes in their working lives. It will be on us as individuals to take our own lead and be ready to keep that one step ahead of the future challenges and changes.

So where does that leave us with our future in health, our ability to function and contribute? As you have just read, with the many generations in the workplace, it then raises the issues of how we will fare in our wellness going forward. I have mentioned previously of our chronic illness and a little about emotional and physical wellness from the anxiety disorders and mental illness challenges people are having, that have yet to really hit the surface in the workplace. It also shows that different generations will have different challenges in their health into the future of the workplace. With all the uncertainty of our workplace and where we might be, how will that affect our health or more importantly, impact on our current health status that will increase the chances of us developing other chronic illness or areas of dementia, depression or anxiety disorders?

When looking back on the history of our labour force in Australia and in comparison, to the research and stats that are put out each year by our Australian Bureau of Statistics, the National health providers in Medibank, HBF, the Australian Institute of Health and Welfare's recent report in 2018, said we are seeing change taking place in what illnesses people had yesterday, today and into the future. I mentioned in the early chapters that chronic illness was of increasing and concerning worry to the community and to the workforce. Up-to-date information from the Australian Institute of Health and Welfare report in 2018, mentioned that the age groups of forty-five to sixty-four years are being challenged with coronary heart disease, lung disease, suicides, breast cancers and colorectal cancers, as the leading areas of death in Australia.

If we look at the age group from twenty-five to forty-four years, the reports are indicating a different response to illnesses and health issues or death. This group is showing data that represents high suicide rates, accidental deaths, land and transport deaths, coronary heart disease and other ill-fated causes. Then if we decide to look a little further down the line to generations of fourteen years old to twenty-four coming into the work force, in some cases are already working part time while they are at high school or will be entrenched in our workplace in the next ten years, we are seeing similar outcomes to the previous age groups and health challenges. They will include suicide, land and transport deaths, accidental poisoning, assaults and other ill-fated deaths.

With that in mind and the ever changing and increase of generations, are we focused more on preparing people for the workplace with education and skilled based learning, or should we also have a balance with more of health and wellness education? With our younger generations facing possible obesity, anxiety disorders, diabetes, mental health issues of relevance to their own situation, if not overcome before entering the workplace, will place a huge cost on our health system and the business sector, and also more importantly, their ability to keep their jobs. Their ability to be physically active and emotionally well with a balanced life style, and to go to their job and enjoy it will be a most interesting journey for both them and the employer.

People will, over various times of their life, experience a range of health problems. As seen in the above, individuals in age categories have shown where the future lies with health. So, will businesses be more conscious of where their future employees stand with their health status? Or will they be ready for the new generations to come with their own forms of illnesses that may impact the workplace? This will, in time, transition to the workplace and it will be up to the individual to either overcome their early health issues or still progressively be working through them. When they hit the workforce, the realisation of how they will work through it emotionally and physically will be the challenge. It will be a test of how they manage their lifestyle, physical activity, home life, social settings, their interaction with the community, or their discipline to studies if that is the first pathway to building a future career.

Businesses are facing their own burdens along the way with their approach to managing and working with their staff. We are seeing businesses looking to be more proactive in providing a suitable environment that everyone can enjoy and be positively productive at the same time. I will go into this more in-depth in Chapter 10 and mention ways that companies are looking to improve and innovate their workplace with a healthy and harmonious approach.

The costs to businesses with insurance claims, worker compensations, workplace harassment, injuries and accidents, and aggressive behaviour all build up with time. Companies are looking to see how they can do business differently, through using more labour hire to get a feel for temporary staff before taking them on full time, and this is not new. They are looking to invest in new market areas that do take time to establish themselves, keeping in the backs of their minds the workforce they have on their hands to work through current projects and have success.

We have seen in recent times in Australia some industries that have suffered greatly with the downturn of mining and construction. This has a flow on effect to other industries and then onto the retail industry, due to people not spending or buying. Where a lot of people are employed, are facing shaky workplace prospects. Fortunately, in Australia there has been a concerted effort by businesses to trade out of tough and financial problems with minimum employment loss, to try and be innovative, develop new products, and ways of cost cutting to prevent the early upsurge of unemployment. When you have uncertainty in the workplace, you have many issues to contend with, and our wellness goes to the top of the ladder as an aspect that will affect everyone at some stage.

In an earlier chapter, I mentioned how our behaviour affects our ability to work and function, be productive and show our brilliance. So how does one get up in the morning, face the day and then come in to work when not feeling on top of the world? The increase in mental health issues in the workplace is gathering momentum and has done so for the past decade. It is, and has been going on, a lot longer than discussed, it has just never been spoken about openly until recent times. For people and businesses to run at their optimum level you need positive all-round health which includes your mental health as well.

When it comes to mental health, it does describe a various range of behaviours and mental disorders. In Australia, the stats show that mental illness is on the incline, and with younger generations coming through and yet to hit the workforce, they will bring along a line of issues with them. The challenge for individuals with mental illness is how long they will endure it, or whether they can overcome it, and if they do improve and slowly make progress, how long will that take. The individuals going through mental illness are themselves feeling left out, disconnected with family, friends and community, having to be on prescribed medicine and then facing financial burdens that just further affects their ability to enjoy some piece of their life.

On top of that, knowing they cannot go to work, where they are able to take part and contribute and feel valued is disempowering. This also has a wide spread effect on their families, spouses and their children, and they feel a loss of self-esteem towards life in general. This then adds to the personal issues of not providing a decent quality of life, not showing up, and once again a disheartening is felt with the experience. At the same time, it is a huge cost to our community and society, with medical expenses and the interruption of a future within the workplace. The increase of depression, dementia and anxiety disorders is reaching all of our current workplace generations, and no one is immune to it.

I have spoken to past work staff of the challenges they have had, one being a 22-year-old female from Perth, named Kristie. She mentioned to me that her workplace supervisor (who was a female) was most aggressive and abusive to her during her shifts. Her work was in the take away food area, where Kristie always felt intimidated and threatened while she was working through her duties. She said that she would be wound up well before coming to work, with a knot in her stomach and ready to be hit by an aggressive supervisor. She said that in turn, it had a tremendous effect on her health which progressively spiralled downwards. She then went to her General Practitioner for medical help to not just get some relief with her emotional and stress levels, but to also find out what she was experiencing with her health.

She was diagnosed with anxiety disorder, and then set about trying to find other work, but that didn't eventuate, so she then opted to quit her job and take time out. But on top of that she still had her financial commitments, and the stress further increased, and was totally lost in all the experience of her un-wellness.

These are common stories, both you and I have heard similar, and you may have even been in that situation yourself. We are most vulnerable us human beings, the pressures of life, our requirements to perform at an optimum level is always expected, and something must give. Invariably it's our health and our ability to maintain wellness.

The workplace right now is seeing many shifts and changes to their workforce in terms of health, and the rise in absenteeism, as discussed previously, creates many obstacles for employers to have a settled and happy workplace. Businesses, whether small or large, take on huge costs and expenses to having their staff off work, with injuries and other related workplace matters that have caused people to miss work.

There are Companies who are always looking to improve their work health and safety systems in place, who check their operations, their compliance, workplace practices, that employment conditions are meeting the standards, and hopefully minimise the short and long-term risks to their business. Then on the other hand, I have spoken to many businesses who have not considered improving their safe working and risks systems or being proactive to training their staff in the awareness of health and behaviour. There is a sense that it 'won't happen to us', or if it is happening to us, we will turn a blind eye and hope it goes away. Speaking to Greg Comans of SAFCOM, one of our leading experts on Safety Risk Management, Perth, Western Australia, said, "Businesses in most cases are waiting for the incident or issues to occur before they do anything about it". He also said, "Some businesses were being proactive, but most are reluctant to invest in their workplace to safety-risk the future wellbeing in the workplace". This is not the first time I have spoken to a Risk management expert or specialist who has also told me the same issues of businesses practices. All these underlying issues in the workplace do change at some stage, as it will catch us out if we do not become involved in it. We do know business is trying to go a thousand miles an hour, but our culture and understanding of the workplace can be improved if we pay attention to the issues that will affect the business and then to the health of the workforce and company too.

If we can be more conscious of the culture, the environment, have well informed tool box meetings and senior managers meet to work out ways of improving our workplace, then the health of people will improve. This will also add value to those that come into the workplace each day who are struggling with health issues that may be turned around with a positive and harmonious workplace environment. It also supports people who have forms of disabilities to be made to feel more inclusive to the workplace and enjoy being involved and not feel out of place.

Our workplace has evolved tremendously in the last ten or twenty years with an incredible acceleration of progress in technology, science, and skills, but not so much with health in the workplace. I will mention that our overall health system and developments or improvement in parts have enhanced our lives. We are living longer, the science of medicine and research has made incredible advances in all forms of health issues and we are seeing many lives saved each day, with medical specialists having a great impact and commitment to people and their future.

I know businesses should not have to take ownership of their employees' lives and wellness, but as they are in the workforce, maybe there are ways we can look to educate, and make aware the possibilities of improving our lives and enjoy being proactive and contributing at the same time. I see this as being a collective or inclusive approach by all parties, to seeing if we can encourage everyone to take care of themselves and encourage each other to greater health. A lot of the health issues out there can be prevented, and the workplace can be one of the vehicles of spreading the good word with the intent of inspiring our whole workforce to participate in the journey of shifting our health in a great new direction.

'There is a sense that it won't happen to us, or if it is happening to us, we will turn a blind eye to it and hope it goes away.'

A Call to Action: Balance your Lifestyle

In this chapter we will discuss various areas of our overall health and wellness, to encourage ourselves to work towards the best possible health we can for the future. It is our current health status that we need to look more deeply into, and see in what ways we can further prevent our chances of increasing the risks to chronic illness, mental illness, and cancer. This is not a subject I am extremely qualified in - the nutritional field - but my whole philosophy and approach in this chapter is to encourage and inspire you to take care of yourselves.

I am sure that if we have not yet experienced poor areas of health or glimpses of illness in our life, that we do know of loved ones and others who are constantly in pain with musculoskeletal issues, with cardiovascular, kidney disease, diabetes, and respiratory to name a few, who would know the personal challenges in working through it.

Our lifestyle has changed in many ways during my lifetime to date. I remember growing up as a teen in the seventies we were all full of activity, and that running around parks, kicking the football, playing cricket, walking to school, and walking into town was a part of our life. There was accessible transport, but mostly my generation preferred to walk if it was twenty or thirty minutes to our destination. We did have high processed foods, and that included starches and sugars, soft drinks, chips, chocolates, cream cakes and lollies that were on offer. But what kept us in reasonable weight and health is that we exercised, we spent late evenings with school friends running around, we drank plenty of water and we had plenty of sunlight.

It was said back in those times that only about seven percent of the youth's population aged between five to 16 years of age were either overweight or borderline obese. The Monash University in 2018, released a report after their studies on six to 13 year olds and the increase in obesity in Australia. It was costing the taxpayers of Australia $43.2 million annually, and that did not include hospital care as well. Monash classified this age group as being an obesity epidemic. The report goes onto to say that one in five children are considered to be overweight or obese. What will our workforce look like in our overall health in the future?

I cannot recall too many people I went to school with that really were overweight or even obese, and if they were, they still took part in some form of activity indoors and outdoors. Being a high school student of the seventies, my school promoted not only good fitness but also good health. I recall in one of my years at Kingswood High School in New South Wales (Australia), we spent a year on our health and learnt about basic areas of the body, how it worked and the types of foods that we should be eating. One thing I will take from those days in school or my youth, was that we had plenty of activity, consumed fewer fatty foods, minimal sugary drinks and a lot of sunlight. I am sure it really helped our health and vitality and aided with stress levels too. I also believe looking back, that it helped us with our attention and concentration with school work and even more when we were doing our grades and exams.

Now we are forty years on and it has all been turned upside down on its head, we are now facing one of the great challenges to our quality of life, the chronic disease of obesity, along with high reported diabetes spreading throughout the community. What is overly concerning, is that earlier I mentioned that seven percent of the youth age group 5 to 16 years in the 1970's was reported to be 7% overweight or obese. We are now being informed that the same age group in 2017 was estimated to be at 27% obese, more so than overweight. Since the seventies, our youth has had an increase in weight gain of three-fold. That is staggering, considering our population in Australia in the mid-seventies was just on fourteen million people and now we have grown to over twenty-five in million in August 2018.

So what affects does this have on our future health? We have a future workforce that will be having challenges in performing to the peak of their talent, with a range of different health issues to the earlier workplace generations.

Now we are seeing businesses in the modern age with better technology and advanced workplace settings looking for those skilled people to complement their workplace and their future. The importance of our workplace environment being able to embrace and provide a harmonising welcome will be paramount, going into the future. There will be a responsible approach by employees to monitor their own health and to ensure they are able to consider their self-care while working. This is a partnership arrangement between the employer and the employee, and if all work together and support each other with a good working environment, all round we will see positive outcomes.

The onus for employers is to understand their staff's current health status and health conditions (if they have one), and how they can manage and work through their issues will be the test of whether they will have a long and productive life in the workforce. Businesses will be encouraged to look at how they are developing their environments, their attitudes towards supporting competent staff, people with disabilities, workplace injuries, and inspiring positive behaviours with ongoing education and awareness.

One of the areas business can encourage staff is through regular activity during the working day. Encourage staff to take that extra walk at lunch time, spending thirty minutes walking and getting some fresh air. The inclusion of activity in our lives is principal to our future wellbeing. In my time as a Myopractor, I was always encouraging people to stay active, to get out in the sunlight as it reduces the stress and anxieties we may experience while working. With a balance nutritional approach and drinking plenty of water, each and every one of us will see the benefits of exercise and activity while we are at work. This also leads to positive connections at work while we develop lunch time walks with friends who are keen to improve, and keep our minds refreshed and stress free. The opportunity to walk in the fresh air only advances our health, and with management and reducing our weight, we start to revitalise our body and to increase its vitality.

The increase and constant exercise or activity will start to reduce the threat of chronic illness. It has been said that seven chronic diseases are linked to inadequate activity such as bowel cancer, diabetes, coronary heart, dementia, stroke, and uterine cancer. Having your body maintained with physical activity and a healthy diet is very central to maintaining your body and energy balance. A terrific way to avoiding being overweight or moving towards obesity. When you progress to an obese stage, it is exceedingly difficult to come back on your own with self-discipline and in most cases, you may need your GP to assist, along with a nutritional expert, and possibly a fitness coach to get you back into good physical shape.

Sitting around in your office is also a start to chronic disease, and we are now seeing office spaces becoming more innovative with energising and uplifting environments. In chapter 10, I will discuss the way buildings are being designed to assist in people's health and improvements. But sitting around is a way to become lethargic, fatigued, and inactive, so it's important to keep moving about, keep the muscles vibrant, get fresh air, drink plenty of water and you will get through the day well, and hopefully enjoyed it too.

I will attest that at one stage I was progressively heading towards an obese state of health. It was out of character for me, to be unfit and carrying a great deal of weight. I had personal issues and challenges going on and became sluggish, tired and fatigued, and my health was rapidly going downhill. The motivating factor for me came when I fell over on the ground and onto my back one day kicking the football with my son. I just couldn't get up. I asked him to come over to me and embarrassingly asked him to give me his hand, so I could get back on my feet. He was only eight years of age at the time, and I have never forgotten that light bulb moment. He and I have spoken about it on the odd occasion since.

Right from that moment, I did decide that I needed to take responsibility and take control of my weight gain. I was also missing my exercises as well, running around and feeling great about being involved in sporting activities. Fortunately, over the next twelve months or so after that event I was able to turn it all around. A lot of hard and consistent work was needed by me, along with watching my exercise patterns and the food and drinks I was consuming. At the end of the day, there were things I was missing out on and the only way to do it was for me to take responsibility and get on with it. Only I could choose to be healthy or least improve my wellness.

Mentally, I am sure it improved my outlook, my ability to function, behave and communicate effectively with others, and maintain a positive and happy life balance. My confidence reappeared, and I felt great being out there mixing it with the community. I will say that I didn't feel depressed but felt an air of embarrassment that I had arrived at that stage in my life of weight gain and poor activity on my part.

One of the other impacts to our diet has been the high increase of sugars in our foods and drinks. The increase over the last twenty or so years has seen our community suffering with regards to chronic diseases, our increase in weight and our ability to recover when we fall ill. We are now in an epidemic of diabetes in Australia.

It was further clear to me when I was a sessional lecturer at Notre Dame University in 2016, delivering a range of health units and assessments to students attending the Broome Campus who were completing units in nursing qualifications. As I mentioned very earlier in my introduction, I am of aboriginal descent, my family are from the East Kimberley region of Gija country. The work I was performing with Notre Dame and in respect to the independent research, is one of my other passions; Foetal Alcohol Disorder Syndrome or better known as FASD. I witnessed more consciously the health and lifestyle of not only Aboriginal people, but also the non-Aboriginal people living in the Kimberley region of WA. The high intake of alcohol, smoking of tobacco, high processed meats and foods that contained high sugars and starch. Soft drinks, fruit juice and energy drinks, along with potato chips and chocolates, are all part of the selections on offer to purchase and are a common food choice.

    I remember sitting and having a pleasant Friday night out in Broome at a popular social venue, looking at the people going about their lives socially connecting. Asking myself, how is it that people can keep this up, eating foods with high processed content and drinking high sugars and alcohol? How is it affecting us? What is it doing to our bodies, how do we recover each day to go to work? Is the nutritional level of food assisting us with imbedding our chronic illnesses, or is it in the development of other pre-illnesses yet to surface? I then asked myself, what effects does this have on our workplace and into the future? Knowing our workplace will be changing and reinventing itself and taking on a new shape into the future, what will this do to businesses in the next ten to twenty or thirty years?

That night of people watching was the trigger for me to write this book. One thing I did conclude was that it didn't matter whether you were living in Broome, my family home town of Halls Creek, or a remote country town of WA or even the Perth metropolitan or other cities, the health of our community in general was doing it tough regardless of where people lived. It was not long after my return to Perth from Broome that I started to spread the word of wellness, its impact, and the risks to our employees and employers and overall progressive workforce.

With the current challenges for people in the workplace that work in an office setting, sitting for extended periods of time, reduced activity, and weight gain that leads to chronic health issues such as heart disease, diabetes and then onto cancer, long working hours creates life balance difficulties. Trying to manage our diet and activity while facing fatigue causes us to eat erratically and spontaneously, and that affects our overall health. But at the end of the day, how much do we want to turn our health around? This can also lead to stress with deciding what is good, what the right thing is to do, and there are many specialists in this field who have many ways to engage their clients to best plan how get you back to good health with a safe, monitored approach.

Education in the workplace to improve people's lives should be further encouraged and provide inspiration to enjoying working towards good health. We are seeing companies provide in-house gym facilities for easy access to staff, bring in professional people to take workers through Tai Chi, Yoga and head and neck massage services, to further reduce the stresses taking place. All these initiatives are a positive step towards looking after its workforce and its business moving into the future.

One of the tips I would like to share with you from a Myopractor's point of view is the value of stretching when you get up in the morning. I would encourage everyone when getting up out of bed each day to stretch for a couple of minutes. Stretching your quads, arms, hamstrings, touching your toes and breathing in and out very slowly. Just a couple of minutes to revitalise the body and incorporate your breathing will, over a period time, reduce muscle injury and stiffness.

Just consider this: if you were sleeping all night and tucked up in bed and sleeping in a foetal position like most of us do at some stage in the night, your muscles will develop tightness due to in-activity. We then have the alarm clock that wakes us up and we jump out bed with no thought to giving the body a chance to wake up. Those couple of minutes of stretching will prevent any further injury, they will start to reduce your current pain for the day, you will feel flexible and nimble, which allows you to get in and out of the car or to the train for work, and any other activity you are required to perform on your feet and with your body. So, take a minute and give yourself that time to invest in you, which helps your day to start off well.

Although I have spent a bit of time focusing on the workplace environment throughout this book, I must tell you, we ourselves need to balance it out too. One of the crucial places for us improving our lives for the workplace is our home. As mentioned in chapter's five and six, we spend just as much time at home as we do at work. Our home is in a lot of ways our sanctuary, a place to get away from the world or a place that does not have happy people living in it. It's so important to enjoy your home space, but it comes with all sorts of challenges. Whether you live alone or in a relationship, whether you have children or not, will add more dimensions.

With the fast paced life we live, always on the go, not only working late but social meetings to attend, sporting associations to part take in, running children to their events, taking part in networking, hanging out with friends, when we don't take time for rest and to reduce stress we get into trouble with our health. We are all subject to the common cold, but when our resistance is down, we are hit with a virus, bug, or health complaint from left field. When we are constantly on the go, we need to be eating right, having quality physical exercise time and getting enough sleep. Otherwise we are more prone to being unwell.

So in future, look at your home environment and find out what is not serving you well and see if you can address it. Only you will know the aspects of your home life and what is affecting you and your health, and whether you are carrying it into your place of work. How much of our peripheral baggage do we bring into work, and is it impacting on our ability to function, concentrate and perform? If we bring stresses, anxiety, ill health, and other connected issues then our day is not off to a good start. Are we then enjoying our workplace? Our health and wellness in most cases begins at the front door of leaving our home, so what happens the moment of walking through the front door of our workplace then?

It's important in a workplace setting that our employers and employees can build an open and honest working relationship together, that reduces any of the stresses and anxiety, and prevents things going to war. To be able to be inclusive and share ideas of how the workplace can be a place for everyone to enjoy and the business to embrace its fellow staff, whom in a lot of ways have great suggestions and ideas for creating a vibrant and heathy place to be. That education on wellness in all its forms is instigated in the workplace and build awareness of programs that could be of great benefit for everyone. That an open dialogue of discussion is tabled regularly with leaders and staff members in the business to be transparent, to keep people informed and encouraged to take care of themselves.

There is no magic wand to improving our lives overnight, but what can be done is to help and share ideas with inspiring encouragement that will, in some way, help people have great lives at work. Right now, people are just getting by, under extreme pain, taking high prescribed pain killers, feeling like emotional wrecks, physically tired and still having to do their work.

There are a lot of factors in our workplace, as explained in earlier chapters, to how our day will work out and if we get through it. Our health is the key to our ability to function and perform, not just relying on a good education or a business network base. We only get one chance at it, so what will you do to kick start your recovery? I want to reassure you to take the lead, inspire those around you, and that by taking small steps you can take back your life and with it, fun and enjoyment. It's the chance you should give yourself. Take that opportunity to value yourself and the health you are fighting for, as you will reap the rewards, I am sure. Best wishes to you.

'In the end, it's how much you want to turn your health around. It is our responsibility to a greater extent at the end of the day.'

The New Frontier of Leadership

In this chapter I would like to focus on the environment in which we live and work. Where in both we spend a great part of our lives, and where we look to experience the benefits in different forms that hopefully brings us countless joys and successes along the way.

It was when I was attending Naturopathy studies in 2013 that I understood how the environment in which we function personally impacted on our ability to heal, to focus, to be productive, of sound and positive health, as well as being mentally well and to be able to ensure our emotional and physical wellbeing stayed in balance. The health philosophy that I understood was that our health outcomes were influenced or governed by our stresses, nutritional intake, and the environment. We do know there are other factors such as where we live, our demographics, our socioeconomics potential, our geographical location (either in the main Cities, regional towns or even our very remote locations), our access to water, essential services and the professions we have taken on as well. Stress, nutrition and our environment is very much a partnership arrangement, whether we be at home, at work, or in a social setting.

Our environment is so crucial to our ability to adapt and function at an optimum level for all round good health, self-growth, and performance. It holds the key (from my perspective) in people having great lives both emotionally and physically. A healthy environment along with good nutritional foods and reduced stress surely will make life far more positive, productive, and enjoyable.

Our environment allows us to build close relationships in the workplace, and with a healthy office, it provides an opportunity for people to enjoy, to feel they are wanted and inspired to arrive each day. It allows us to mingle and socialise, which provides a place to share ideas, discuss internal business and to enhance our ability to contribute without fear. A lot of workplace environments do the opposite to this and portray fear, ego and a controlled approach, a 'will do' approach, which at the end of the day doesn't bring out the best in people, it only further imbeds the issues, and people become unwell and decide to either not come to work or resign. What does this effect have on business moving into the future, with their employees not feeling as though they are contributing and producing something meaningful?

Now back to the focus of this chapter. How can we embrace a positive workplace environment that brings vitality and inspiration that allows great people and company values to align, to share success and take away the unnecessary stress? This all forms part of our continual improvement towards good health in the workplace. Regardless of our positions, leadership roles, our ability to connect and behave professionally, having authentic discussions around building workplace relationships is paramount to long term prosperity.

Our environment is made up of people of various ages, different life experiences, short and long employment at the workplace, varied qualifications and different beliefs and values. Having to deal with their internal health and peripheral challenges adds to an interesting experience for each of us. Whenever I feel good, of healthy mind, invigorating energy, being encouraged to be inclusive and to contribute, is when I am at the top of my work game and my enthusiasm levels just rise to the top. I guess one of the essences of my aims is that I want autonomy in my work and in the future. There are many that share the same view and do it too.

Another area in our workplace that needs focus and continual development is in the behaviour of staff and businesses with one another. I did spend more in-depth time on workplace behaviour in chapter 7, but it is most relevant to the building and fostering of our environment. Invariably when you mix toxicity, negativity and poor behaviour in the environment, the atmosphere produces all sorts of non-productive, egotistical vibes, and uneasiness that is pulling the organisation and people apart. One of the areas that is ever so consistent is the inconsistencies there are in the workplace. There is still a behaviour of 'do as I say and not as I do'. We still see this not only being played out in the small and large companies, but in very high corporate and even in government sectors. When we see inconsistencies in the workplace, trust is the first thing that goes out the window. Once trust goes, it's extremely hard to earn it back to the same level it once was. There will always be uncertainty and doubt, some issues can be mended, but in most cases, caution is the first line of attack and defence when further decisions or directives are given. It is these areas of life that starts to affect people in their work and could be the trigger for onset of their illness or influence further their health problems.

I see with the ever-changing workplace a new form of leadership needs to occur, not just through inclusiveness of staff and business, team building, problem solving and creative thinking strategies, but more to the understanding of our business community and to the future of staff welfare. We do know that business is under threat, and needs to be consistently innovating and marking their potential to stay in the market place nationally or globally. However, we do need more investment towards how we can manage and work with our staff and their issues of health. Many staff who are challenged with illnesses as discussed in earlier chapters felt most uneasy to confront their supervisors, managers or HR Department and explain their circumstances. These are people who have great talent and produce work of the highest standard. In most cases, they feel if they do have an issue it will be met with a vague response that could put their position in jeopardy.

We do know that our workplace has changed with areas in our stereotyping, with more inclusion of staff with disabilities. It is one of the more inspiring moves that has happened in our workplace. Our community who have disabilities are able to participate, be included equally and valued in their contribution and along with themselves feeling they are giving invaluable input to the workplace. The increase of disability employment in the last five to ten years in Australia, and still on the increase, is astounding. We are, and need to be, an inclusive and equal opportunity workforce, that values everyone and provides a safe place for all concerns.

Another incredible growth to our workplace environment is the change in the last thirty years of our diverse cultures into Australia. Going back to the early to mid-eighties, we had approximately fifty or so diverse cultures and we now have in 2018 around four hundred or more. Our community has expanded and grown tremendously, with now a reported population in August of over twenty-five million people in Australia in 2018. I know there are still some challenges out there, but there is a great effort by the community to work and understand we are all here and that we must try to build solid and enjoyable relationships. I know from an Aboriginal perspective, I have great friends from all diverse backgrounds, where I socially play sport, network in business, and maintain social catch ups without really giving any thought to the colour of their skin or country they come from.

What has been enlightening in our ever-increasing diverse cultures coming to Australia, is how well they have adapted and are ready to participate in being part of a workplace team. Over my working life, the high level of skills and creative thinking from diverse people who have entered our workplace is very noticeable. With the changing workplace of where business and people will go into the future along with a more diverse community, there will be challenges along the way. I am sure Industry, Governments, Businesses or Corporate Companies will work through these into the future. But they will need to look at their role in providing a workforce that engages wellness, with education and awareness. With an increasing workplace will come more challenges to health, more costs to insurance, worker compensation claims, legalities, and liabilities. Now is the time for businesses and our workers to consider our health and wellbeing.

We do not know where we will be in the next twelve months, five years or twenty years from now in fact. But we do know that change will be inevitable, and our health in all forms will be tested and challenged if we don't take care of ourselves. We only have one life and it is our responsibility to look after ourselves and encourage our families to do the same. At the end of the day, to do something positive if we intend to stick around and play a part in the workforce. In most cases, we cannot change the world, but we can change our own health and be more preventative. This will also provide us with other opportunities to take on new roles that previously we thought we couldn't have tried before. But making a conscious decision to consider our wellbeing and to improve our vitality can lead us to another great adventure in the workplace.

I have mentioned so far in this chapter a couple of variables to our workplace environment changes. One area I feel is important to discuss is the physical environment we work in. We talk about the environment of people and the attitudes and behaviours that are engaged in, but the physical environment also needs to have a balance within our functioning behaviour when we are at work.

To begin with, since the 1970's our physical workplace has changed to what we are now experiencing. The workplace has changed in the way more people are working, our population has increased by eleven million people in the last forty years, businesses are doing business more differently, diversely and globally, its 24/7, and the inclusion of high technology, internet and advanced communications has seen the transformation from being in an office where people would meet, to skyping from all parts of the world, which provides others to attend online meetings of convenience. We are seeing businesses restructure their workplace to alternative approaches of staff working from home and other incubator type offices, that reduce costs and create more effective ways to operate a business.

Before we delve a little more into this, let's take a quick snapshot of our past and bring it forwards to today. When I started in the workforce at the end of 1980, it was quite different to now. There was an introductory to innovative technology, computers, and the commencement of Auto Teller Machines, as my first job was working in the bank. The evolution of change since that period to now has been unbelievable. Our offices were like the culture of offices in other industries that included cubicles, where employees were required to work independently and stay focused on the work. We were also less 'tech leaning' even though it was subtly being brought in, and at the time, were instructed with the new machines and with training. There were still forms of communications of telexes, telegrams that would be delivered by the postman. We all used landline telephones as the hint of mobile phones wasn't evident in those early days. We all used diaries to note our meetings and appointments through hard copy journals.

It's funny when I look back at how we used to make long term appointments verbally, either at the workplace or in social settings, how we always remembered them and nine times out of ten, the people would meet at the times appointed. Nowadays we use our mobile calendar to remind us. We then moved through the eighties into the nineties and the pace began to pick up with technology, we were introduced to the internet and mobile phones were becoming all the rage. Our workplace was using the facsimile to send information or copies of documents to one another, more up-to-date business communications systems took over the phone landlines as mobile phones started to take over progressively. The introduction of email, the word processor, and our own first computers brought a new dimension to our workplace, and I dare say, a whole lot of new stresses with understanding the change in our workplace technology. I, for one, was always as nervous as anyone to try and use the technology, but over time I did improve and accepted that it was part of the future or I would be left behind.

From the beginning of 2000, there was a more settled period for staff now having become used to using the up-to-date technology. There was a big effort by everyone to up-skill themselves and become more confident with the arrival of technology. But the stress levels remained on the rise, there were more deadlines to meet, businesses were enjoying a new time of technology advancement but the employees felt like they were working overtime, their hours increased, and pressure was mounting.

It was around this period I saw new areas of health and wellness start to decline as the stress levels were increasing. I had a labour hire company around that time in the early 2000's, and I did see evidence that our mental health issues could become a future challenge. But through our two thousand year period, we did see the rise of, and other adaptions to, technology, Social Media, Twitter, Facebook, and video link ups that became part of our community and the workplace.

What has progressed since and more so in the last five or so years, is the way buildings are designed for the workplace. To make them easier, friendlier and to encourage a place to be appreciated. We are seeing how buildings are now designed and built with health in mind. In the past, our workplace has seen a sizable portion of our workforce working indoors. Invariably, when working indoors we are lacking natural sunlight, not drinking enough water and air circulation is limited.

What we are now seeing is a more concerted effort for buildings to include more natural sunlight and easy access to water filtrations to ensure staff keep up hydration that keeps our bodily functions and temperature in homeostasis state. The temperature, the air circulation, is now being monitored to every square metre of the building to ensure that air is meeting requirements and adjusted to meet the demands of the area of the workplace floor. This is to ensure people are comfortable while they are working, while keeping it environmentally friendly. This in turn reduces high absentee rates, staff turnovers, burnout and provides an environment that happily engages the workplace.

The designing of office space or buildings have included other innovative ideas to improving the workplace with quality lighting, bringing the outdoors to the indoors with plants, artificial grass, forest, and plantation landscapes to revitalise the workplace. The implementation of large windows, to bring in the natural light, will look to reduce fatigue and apathy in work performance. The inclusion of stand-up working desks has appeared more so than ever. Just recently, a study by Deakin University was conducted in which more than 230 workers took part, to sit less and move more, with added health coaching strategies to assist the workers at their workplace. The study indicated that if more employees were to adopt a more 'stand up' and 'sit less' approach in the workplace, the savings to our health would be substantially reduced in the long run. This is all part of the preventative approach to reducing obesity and related diseases, Deakin University said.

We are now seeing a more open approach to meetings being held either in open glass offices where people can see in and out, or by taking walks outside if weather is permitting to have meetings to get some fresh air and use the time to increase activity and exercise out of the office. New building approaches to designing ecofriendly workplaces have provided people the use of gym equipment if available on site to increase their exercise, and there has been a significant increase in staff now using stairs instead of lifts to go to meetings and briefing upstairs in their buildings.

There have been the introduction of rooms provided for staff to refresh with a short siesta, small sleep time rooms to relax and gather themselves while at work. Some businesses and corporate companies have included (some time ago) the availability of a head and neck massage facilitator to come into the workplace every couple of weeks to further relax and reduce the tension around the cervical region with all staff. Along with those supports, we are seeing employees bringing Yoga and Tai Chi, which improves breathing and respiratory systems techniques, and Pilates to assist in the strengthening of the muscular and body flexibility, to reduce workplace incidents and accidents and which also reduces those potential issues of aches and pain into the future. Especially around the lower lumber areas of the back where there is a high portion of the working population experiencing all forms of issues and pain and discomfort.

The advantages of incorporating a new approach to building designs for employees is to take health into greater consideration in the workplace. It also does wonders for improving stress and anxiety levels. The reduction of poor behaviour and communications in the workplace, with the added approach of implementing regular activities such as gyms and open air approaches is having a great effect on reducing absenteeism and illness, as they might have been before. What this also does is to ensure the workplace is a comfortable atmosphere, with a new layout of office furniture that is more energised and provides a place to be positively productive at the same time. It may not erase the individual health issues one may face but there is a significant effort for the designs of the building to embrace the staff and make it more comfortable while at work.

Herein lies a question. If our workplace is contributing to some of our unhealthy outcomes with our personal health, then what is our home environment like? We will spend a great deal of our life in the workplace and with long hours of commitment. Is then our home environment affecting our health too? Are there areas of your home space that's not helping your health positively? With all the home renovations projects people have put themselves through over the last ten years, has it impacted positively, revitalised your health or has it just made your chronic illness even more challenging or created other unfortunate illness to appear? Or, is that why you decided to renovate, to bring great wealth of health and enjoyment to you and your family to make that change?

Our wellness will be challenged depending on the environment we spend time in. It will be governed by our environment along with the behavioural energy around us, such as a toxic relationship or non-productive communications. Or the other side of the coin, the love, peace and harmonious attitude that brings great inspiration and goodwill with it. Consider your health and the value your environment is giving you, and whether it is serving you well and being healthy at the same time. Do not forget to invest in yourself, take care of your nutritional intake, enjoy the natural sunlight, reduce the stresses and anxieties, drink plenty of water and get out for a walk. You will start to see great new changes to your health - you deserve it!

'Our environment is so crucial to our ability to adapt and function at an optimum level for all round good health, self-growth and performance. It holds a key in people having great lives both emotionally and physically.'

The Impact of Workplace Culture

The progression of unacceptable behaviour within our workplace culture is coming at great cost to the workplace and the community. Not only through Workers Compensation claims, litigation and law suits, businesses are at their wits end to work through issues of poor behaviour. The impact of our health in enduring this form of behaviour, having to experience it over a lengthy period of time, and then having to address it and to come to some resolution can be a time draining journey. Everyone will react emotionally and physically, and then our mental state of processing will create a new dimension to the event. It has long been seen as a major issue for all parties in the workforce; businesses, employees, governments, industries, all generations of employees and those youths looking to enter the workplace.

I continually read newspaper articles every week, press releases, and have private friends sending me clippings from journals and books relating to meagre behaviour of other people's stories. I also have people telling me their own experiences of non-productive en masse workplace behaviour complaints. You only have to read the Chamber of Commerce of Western Australia's Business Pulse publication in April 2018, which spoke of an increase in violence and aggression in the workplace. I mentioned it briefly in the early part of this book. To recap, I mentioned the increase of twenty five percent in the last five years of aggression and bullying in the workplace. The statistic was initially provided by WorkSafe WA based on the compensation claims of incidences taking place in the workplace.

I have been facilitating in this area for almost ten years, there has been a rapid rise in the workplace of behavioural and poor language use, bullying along with aggression, plus the inclusion of using social media to get our dirty washing out or cyberbullying. It tells us a lot about where we are as a society and where we are going if we don't do something about it or come up with a solution for reducing it. There is so much said, discussed, and experienced, and yet we continue to go down the pathway of mistreatment towards one another.

At the end of the day, I am in control of my behaviour, I will have to deal with what I am feeling and reacting to, and how I communicate that will have a result or an outcome that will either be received well or not so well. Is our behaviour a delayed reaction to unresolved issues of the past, with our family upbringing, not having our way at school, being the odd one out or just wanting to be a total control freak?

In a lot of workplaces, we hear of people identified by other staff members by history and past experiences they have endured but nothing gets done about it. Invariably people who are on the wrong end of it are in fear of saying or approaching their supervisor, manager, or HR Department due to being ostracised in the future. Businesses must take the lead role, you are employing people, it's not about building your reputation, your profile or image that's important but building a prosperous team, inspiring your people so they respond to your needs and this will bear the fruits for everyone.

We have seen an increase in the workplace of harassment and bullying, and its effect on people's health and wellbeing. Where these forms of behaviours are increasing, one comes to work filled with anxiety and stress that impacts their ability to function, concentrate on their work, engage with staff members and give the feeling of happiness about their inclusion in the workplace. Instead we find that underneath the surface they are traumatised by unsavoury acts of un-pleasantries towards them. In a lot of cases these acts of incidences don't get reported or verbally mentioned, and we only find out the person has been on the receiving end of the treatment when they've decided it's time to look elsewhere for another job with not a word of why they left.

In the time I have been conducting my programs of Human Behaviour Excellence programs in the Workplace, I have had many stories related to me of instances of aggressive and passive behaviour. It's just not one industry that is the culprit, it's across the board. Many of these industries in some ways portray an upfront environment that welcomes and engages people in having an enjoyable future pathway to employment success. But it is not until you dig down into the business and ethics towards their staff that you get the picture, and that all of the unpopular forms of behaviour is present in the workplace. You only have to speak to your friends and associates to know our workplace is under siege with poor behaviour. It's not just the employees, businesses too are subjected to bad behaviour, with staff not playing their part and putting the business under extreme pressure and risks, both financially and with reputation.

It's through these stories that were shared in my programs, either in front of other participants in the room or shared privately, that I have been able to weave my programs to fit and open up the challenges that exist in the workplace, and to see if we can reduce the behaviours that are not so positively embracing. Right now, at this minute, we have people who are in deep anxiety and stress in the workplace, who are feeling incredible pressure with intense negative behaviour towards them that is becoming a gut-wrenching experience. This is furthering the demise of their health, with the fearful experience placed on them, which only increases and intensifies. Unable to say anything makes it even more difficult to come to work. If in the case of the person who is the victim or discriminated against does take the step forward to management and informs them of the actions against them, we would hope that they are achieving positive resolutions to their issues, that their health is monitored, and any further personal discomforts are reduced. But that is not always the outcome.

What happens after a complaint has been raised? In high profile or large corporate environments there is generally a review, and in a few words, I will map out the process. It commences with where the problem is and where is started, how long it's been going, what has taken place to raise the review, who may be involved, and where and what steps are needed to rectify the problem and resolving it to then move forwards. The general term used out there is it's 'the culture of the workforce' that's impacting on people and the business. Independent consultants are brought in to review the grievances and complaints made by a staff member/s or the company itself.

One of the practices in the initial stages of a review is to send out a survey or a questionnaire to get a feel for the culture and the atmosphere of how people are feeling about their workplace. This is to draw people to confidentially raise issues relating to morale, confidence in the environment, any misconduct that may not have been identified earlier, or other harassments or bullying experiences that have not been noted or raised prior to the review. These reviews can take a period to gather the findings, and then they release actions and plans moving forwards along with what will be corrected and how the business will be operating in the future. No doubt issues of poor staff behaviour will be addressed, and there will be implementations of training of staff to rekindle confidence with the organisation. All of this will have high costs associated with having a review of a poor culture within a business. The stress and the illness continues to fester as people are working through their own health issues that in some way has been triggered by the events leading up to the actions towards them in the workplace that has led to the review.

The term toxic is used more so now than ever in describing how a workplace is functioning both positively and negatively. The characteristics of a toxic environment may include; gossip or office politics, feeling imprisoned and unable to break free, forms of manipulation that serves no workplace in development and self-growth, and the environment lacking harmony and confidence. We also see forms of harassment and discriminatory behaviour slipping through the cracks, comments about gender and diverse cultures, not of any constructive language use.

We are finding that it doesn't have to be just verbal expression that affects our workplace but more of the emails crossing here and there, sending discrete messages to share about work colleagues, and texting to one another. This is only the tip of the iceberg, and I am sure as I go through these points you will be familiar with these behaviours in any or all of your previous workplace experiences.

Let's talk about cyberbullying for a moment, as it has been in the increase. As we know, there has been a dramatic rise in our ability to comment and disclose information about people and their movements, about companies and what they do, and to also make comments about what's happening on social media in vehicles. It is no different from the workplace, repeatedly we are seeing comments made that have no positive intent to inspire, to leave a legacy of note that will help our workplace community. We have new generations coming into the workplace, and there are concerns that the school environment will transform or escalate cyberbullying in the future.

There have been numerous articles and whispers in my work, with people and businesses saying this will be having an influence on our workplace going into the future. It appears the culture has been set from our youths entering the workplace and it will just be a normal crossover of behaviours that will be brought along. We know of horrendous outcomes to youth cyberbullying in the past, and if the message is that this is where we are heading, then we will have an out of control workplace. Let me say, I am a great supporter of the younger generations. I have a son who only left high school twelve months ago, and has shared with me events and stories that are most frightening and disturbing. We need to engage with our new incoming workforce to encourage a new way of language use and how that can impact in the changing workplace environment.

At the human Behaviour Excellence Centre, we spend a great deal of time helping and making aware to our participants the use of language, and how that can affect ourselves, the workplace, the team, and the company. We are promoting enriched and positive language and behavioural changes that in the end will impact on everyone in the business, irrespective of whether it the owner, CEO, Supervisor, or the frontline staff member. A shift in behaviour and attitudes to get an engaging and wholesome outcome is what we want in our delivery programs.

Let me share with you one of the approaches we take at Human Behaviour Excellence Centre of GP Bridge Training and Development, to improving workplace behaviour and then to encourage everyone in the workplace to be open minded for change. More so, that people need to acknowledge they may need to be conscious of their doings along the way. Initially when we start our programs it's all based around our language use. We are seeing evidence of language behaviour being sent out on all forms of the cyberspace via Facebook, Twitter, and Instagram and the like, with incredible speed and travel. The effects of our language will tell us a lot about how people are feeling, how they respond to information and how they will react. Our language use via the forms of communications just mentioned is showing a lot of non-productive and self-destroying ways in which we see ourselves. It's not just one generation, it's shared very evenly amongst all the generations out there. As discussed earlier, our high profile and leaders of our community are just as vulnerable to sending out a message of non-value or non-inspiring response or content.

The opportunity for us to consider our language use before we communicate is in our hands, whether it will be received well or not so well. The next time you use Twitter, Facebook, texting, or exchanging emails, have a look at your language use and see if it is of great value to you and the receiver of them. What is our aim in sending out a message of aggression, bullying or defamatory remarks, what is the desired result we want, are we looking for a reaction or validation, what do we hope to achieve from it? In the workplace we are seeing an increase in poor language use that is most traumatising to a co-worker or the team. It's time for businesses and workplace employees to consider their language use more professionally and constructively, and with some positive intent. It does nothing to your place of work if language and threats are bounding around destroying the environment and unsettling the great human spirit of people.

In brief, language can be looked at in two ways; the empowerment or disempowerment of language. If we break that up and ask people in the workplace what is the language they would most be inspired by, it would be the empowerment language. That would be words that are positive, that foster high self-esteem, that encourage people to enjoy coming to their work and the companies get a benefit from having a workplace that thrives on wholesome involvement.

The reputation and image of the organisation or employees only strengthens when you have a happy workforce, which in turn means having a happy customer in the future. The word spreads when people work in a company that is looking after each other and treats people with great human spirit. I do mention the human spirit a few times in this book, as I want to encourage people to be more mindful of each other. Some years ago I worked with a general manager and he showed what great human spirited approaches to our self and to our team of colleagues could do if we stick together and support and inspire. Regardless of our situation, the opportunity to build relationships and have trusted conversations is necessary in building ourselves and others around us. He would say great things came from slow progressive steps that would mount up at the end, then you bring people along that further grows their lives, and if we do that, we will conquer all challenges. That still remains in my head to this day. Thanks Rob McCarthy.

Then you look at the opposite side of the coin, of the non-empowering language use. More and more we see that it has no place for building and enhancing relationships. Everyone now on social media can provide feedback of rage, make discriminatory comments, tell tales about other people, criticise a person or a business's character or profile, and the list goes on. But this is also happening in our workplace, it is coming at a cost in many ways from individual employees to companies in some shape or form through litigation, laws suits, insurance claims, workers compensation, and assault charges. But underneath the surface our health is taking a big hit once again within the workplace, with specific employees or by a business approach or attitude that further impacts with soul destroying outcomes.

Human Behaviour Excellence programs get down to the bottom of it, and informs people of what our actions and consequences have in the workplace. It will have a long-lasting effect on both employees and the employer once we are aware and conscious of our behaviour. It can be a slow road to progression and learning, but it will provide people with tools to overcome, and knowledge that they too can pass on to others. It's also about improving and engaging our workplace and to reduce the unwanted stresses and potential illnesses that affects everyone going forwards.

If businesses and employers want to advance their quality of life, they need to take hold of the reins. Everyone's reputation and longevity are on the line. We are now in the world of showing up and being accountable and competition has never been so fierce to stay in the market place and to keep our jobs. Everyone's behaviour is being seen more than ever, and we not only want strong policies and procedures of business ethics and behaviour to support our businesses, but also our employees. We also need strong behavioural changes in all forms of the workplace that engages, encourages and brings people together, and hopefully great outcomes arise from it.

We have a duty to inspire the younger generations of the power of language and language responses, that if used positively and is embracing in the workplace, will filter out into our social and private lives and improve our relationships. They too, will, in the future, face their own health challenges, but creating a place of great harmony will ease the potential for them to experience forms of illnesses that will impact on their future in some way. It may not fix our health issues, but it will go a long way to enjoying our work and our environment. We need the leaders of this country to be more Statesman-like and not enter into gutter talks about each other that only just divides people and avoids mending and healing relationships.

If we can begin to reassess our language use, and how it's best used to reach our outcomes, then choosing the words and behaviours with it is going to be the first stage to building our reputation and image, which is primary to our future employment and business opportunities we leave behind in our legacy. I guess the question to ask is, what is your workplace culture like? Does it need attention? Does your workplace need to address the following or are you content everything is moving along nicely?

• Reducing and shifting undesirable behaviour and use of language in the workplace

• Understanding the consequences of poor and non-productive language use in all forms (written, verbal and messaging etc.)

• Reduce aggression, bullying and other practices

• Reduce potential workers compensation claims, and legal and litigation risks to the company

• Instigate steps to how business recovers from ethical and behavioural future failures

• Improve company health and employee's personal health in the workplace that improves self-esteem and vitality

The above points are relevant, as businesses will be in a position (if they are committed) and along with their employees, to improve their environment. In the end, our health in many ways is paramount to having a successful workplace for both employee and employer. If we want to move on into the future and take our younger generations along, wouldn't it be great to pass the baton, so they can learn from our experiences and shape the world into a better place, and along the way take care of our health and wellbeing? That's what I would hope would happen.

'The effects of our language used will tell us a lot about how people are feeling, how we respond and how we will react.'

In Closing

Now that we have come to the last chapter and having given you a brief overview of what I have observed, experienced, disclosed or referenced and where we may possibly go into the future. There are still exciting times ahead and not without its challenges to our functional behaviour in a social, family or professional life. Our working and professional lives will take on new shapes and forms as we move through our day to day lives. I don't have answers to the world, but only to say we do have the opportunity with our lives to own it and determine where we would like to end up. I am curious though that with little tweaks here and there, open minded approach and of self-awareness our lives can be fulfilling and prosperous. To think at the end of the day in our health status, we can prevent most of our illnesses and function at a level that in turn gives great quality of life to us and others.

Just to recap on the pages before, our workplace is in some ways could be our only our sanctuary to display or show our best work. If you consider the effort and time you put into investing in yourself to skilling and building your knowledge cannot be denied. It would be a great shame that the investment in yourself goes unnoticed, that your willingness to strive for excellence and inspiration will at the end of the day is rewarded. Through our lives of working long hours, to satisfy our needs and others and the workplace to end up in a lot of ill health is no positive outcome. We also need to see our workplace inspire and provide great vitality to engaging and connecting with the human spirit and that everyone also feels valued and empowered to making an end result worthwhile.

Our workplace culture is so paramount to our long-term gevity to survival. The attitudes to having a balanced approached that invites wellness and good spirited behaviour will in turn see great growth and prosperity. The environment in the workplace is so important to reducing the poor behaviours and aggression to one another. The workplace and everyone all have a stake in it to improve and bring the positive intent out in everyone. I firmly believe with all the work I have done and seen and spoken to people about that if we get our environment right in the workplace we will start to see great shifts in our poor behaviour and above all improved health outcomes. I also see that with our health, that if we work, live and socialise in positive environments and not the toxic scene we will also become more well. We are seeing in companies today, as I have already indicated our workplaces are revisiting their approach to have ecofriendly workplace environments. There is also more attention to organisation to using health and wellness programs to improve the outlook of the company and their employees. But more needs to happen in changing the toxic behaviours and emotional methods of fear, ego and control practices. Instead of using a band aid method of she'll be right mate, but until the environment is focused on and pealed back rid of the unhealthy attitudes and behaviours not serving everyone, we will continue to have the unsavoury issues fester and deeper.

When the workplace loses focus on their most important resource in the human spirit, you first start to reduce your capacity to grow, develop and maintain your existence. Along with fun, enjoyment, then productivity and output begin to affect our future in the business marketplace, notwithstanding the competitiveness of the staying in business and maintaining your hold in operating. It makes it a very challenging experience. We do know and aware of as well that in the business world which is now a global warfare of competitive markets and innovations to stay on top, businesses are looking for the best people to advance themselves in moving forward. It should be encouraged for businesses to go beyond the limit and explore the unknown as this also has a tremendous effect on people to also looking beyond the horizon themselves and see what they can achieve, strive for new explorations, be daring and bold thinking at the same time. Along with the heavy commitment to succeed and be part of the changing shape of our business world, the implementation of improve technology, the urgency to perform at the optimum level, to increase our skill level, be that X factor that will assist in breaking new grounds will have a price at the end of it I am sure, will it be our health that impacts or suffers through it if we don't attend to it or conscious thought to it. With all the stresses of businesses keeping their operations functioning with through technology change, price and market challengers, industry methods dying, to looking for new ways to promote stay ahead of the pack the pressure and financial requirements continue to impact not only financially but also our emotional wellness in the workplace environment.

With added pressure to our intense and competitive world we need to harness and take care of ourselves. Just a reminder to my early point in this book, right now Australia chronic illness is the main cause of deaths. It is estimated that 7 out of 10 deaths in Australia and or related disease and cancers. Those chronic illnesses include cardiovascular or heart disease, diabetes, kidney disease, respiratory, cancers, musculoskeletal system arthritis, respiratory, cancers, a huge rise in obesity. I guess the question I would like to ask is, is there a case to say or investigate whether the workplace is a cause of one of our 7 deaths a year with all the stresses combined and aligned with possible chronic illnesses. But what's the sad fact about it is that we can prevent most of our illnesses and to have our workplace be a possible high cause or influence on our chronic illnesses outcomes and be that at the end it takes my own life is something I did not sign up for.

With our health being challenged and having great effects on our ability to get up each morning getting out of bed then off to work, we then face work with seeing an uprising in our responsiveness to poor behaviour, bullying, aggression, for which we see high absenteeism through, low self-esteem, fatigue, poor concentration, mental health responses and those peripherals of our current life's challenges only impacts on our ability to perform and enjoy our place of work and socially with friends and family. The deterioration of our quality of life and emotional wellbeing can be a long and lasting experience leading into the future.

The pressures of our workplace and the demands to performing and meeting deadlines and on top of that having the pressure of the fear, ego and control methods of behaviour is only going to cause great impacts to the future functioning of productivity and enjoyment in our work. I have not spoken of in the book of the second layer in secrets, lies and betrayals in depth at this stage. I feel this is an area of suppressive behaviour that grinds people to their knees. I have seen and experienced ruthless examples to the workplace displaying these traits with incredible negative self-destruction emotional non-productive outcomes. I believe companies and employees need to visit this area of behaviour and see what it's doing to their business and their staff environment. The environment is a major key to businesses and people having flourishing results if steered down a visionary and productive road and with great trust and value to one another then success is experienced by all. But business and workplace staff always need to examine their role and behaviour more consciously. It doesn't matter which industry or profession, whether it's in the political field, corporate, small business enterprises, our social setting or in the community we still see a dictatorial and authoritarian approaches with mean spirited intention behind the scenes with hidden agendas. Workplace environments playing people off on one another to get a selfish outcome that tears the organisation apart and manipulates the environment for self-gratification is not an ethical process to venture down.

What possess people and businesses to function in this manner and what do they get out of it. Greed and personal vanity are wrapped up behind it, then a lot of others around bare the brunt of behaviour that only intensifies the health issues and people simply don't want to come to work. I have seen the secrets, lies and betrayals work effectively in families to maintain control and I have certainly witnessed these traits portrayed in the workplace to see great talent walk out the door. So, let me ask you a couple of questions, have you ever experienced this form of treatment in the workplace, how did it feel and what was the outcome, did you reach a positive resolve. Or have you every influenced your behaviour to get an upper hand on someone with unfair play, to use your position that boarded on line with bullying and aggression and how did that feel, and did you reach the outcome you were looking for. Only you can be the judge here. But it's a sad day when we see positions of negative behaviour expressed for our own gain and in the mean time we destroy people's goodwill and good intent.

Given that its estimated by the Forbes magazine in 2013, saying almost 90% of the American workplace population are not enjoying, being happy, feeling frustrated while they are working. In Australia, we may not be too far behind in those outcomes to workplace practices that show unfair communications and behaviour going from the increasing reports to bullying and aggression on the rise in all industries. Now we are in 2019, I have spoken to many people and they have given feedback in some form, its telling me that those statistics are increasing as the years move on in the workplace. Something has to give in our wellness to function our health with stresses, anxiety, chronic illnesses, depression, our increasing consumption of medication, poor nutritional lifestyles will just continue to compound our capacity to get through the day before we can start to consider our roles in the family and other personal responsibilities.

What is concerning is the increase of mental health issues of stress, anxiety stress disorder, post-traumatic stress disorder in our public service people. We are seeing an escalation of rise in such areas in our police services, armed forces, nursing and health professionals, fire services, ambulance services, prisons services and the education sector the list goes apart from those other industries where employment is crucial to people's wellbeing. That are experiencing incredible emotional burn out and physical unwellness. This is something not new, in fact I believe it's been in our workplace for hundreds of years and previously not either taken seriously or just plain naivety to the fact we are all told to 'suck it up princess', but its hitting our community in one form or another at an incredible rate, with good people not feeling wellness. Attitudes have changed its more acknowledgement and concerns have seen it been instigated for action in working with and looking to better ways to understanding and how best we communicate mental health, it's a priority driven now. But it is now, many of those services just mentioned are roles where by people go into places of battles, areas of the known in when they are called upon to then face a scene of traumatise eventful experience.

I can't begin to know what our services people encounter and how they can begin to rationalise their emotional responses after the event when placed in a most difficult and life-threatening scene. They not only do it on one occasion but time and time again going to a place of chaos and madness with incredible courage, so they can ensure lives are safe and looked after. Its these traumatic understandings our frontline people put their training and knowledge to the test and when all said and done are the ones that suffer the consequences of ill health and poor quality of life without considering their professional work future going out the door. They are human after all, they think, feel and internalise, they self-judge themselves 'if they could have done it differently', wear the scars of the moment and for rest of their lives.

Our health is paramount, we are all vulnerable to traumatic and incidents that impact on us and in some way, we may never recover from it. To have these experiences further compact on our existing health illness doesn't go to well for us having a great life of pain and sickness. The impacts to our service people on the line of duty at the end can mean leaving their chosen professional passion. The truth be known in most cases they have internalised their beliefs of wanting to stay involved in their work, not letting people know of their emotional illnesses, being disengaged in their workplace which is further impacted by not sharing and being support by their departments then only hits them more and just compounds their mental illness stage. We all know of people closely associated to us who are experiencing this form of dark period in their life. Fortunately, organisations such as Beyond Blue, Headspace in Australia and others are making incredible head ways into supporting and encouraging people with mental illness. Companies and the workforce are now uniting more and more to helping our injured and traumatise colleagues.

Its just not the area of public services, we are all possible and susceptible causalities in experiencing further health complication with induced peripherals of life experiences as mentioned in chapter 6. Our lives away from our work have continual influences to trigger off our health issues or to intensify them. The outside personal factors of relationship break downs, financial challenges, illness of loved ones impacts, continual family factions, pressure to meeting the needs of others when not well, personal legal and law suit battles, to be a day carer for your spouse, concerned for your loved ones in Age Carer locations is most stressful, being a parent to your children, losing of a loved one and many others only increases the health and stress in our lives. We are seeing information overload, more of us having to function at an optimum level that just cuts to the core of our ability to just get through each day. I know of many people who are right now, feeling incredible pressure to perform and show they are bullet proof and are ashamed to show any signs of weakness and emotional responses. In most cases all they are doing is storing it up ready to explode and eventually vent their feelings and their health status both emotionally or physically expressions will come to the surface in some form. All this is a great burden on our ability to function and enjoy life and to further have it impact in the workplace on adds to the plight that that's life. Our workplace environment is such a key for people to remain in a positive wellness state.

Our workplace can be in most cases a place for people to escape from their personal lives and commitments to get a breather from it. Our workplace is where we can all shine, give our best and display our talent and feel valued and acknowledged. But that is not always the case. Our workplace environments needs a new shift in how it manages and communicates for an all-round positive outcome. This is not about the employer having to take full responsibility, wear the costs and the result of toxic culture, our workforce has to rise above and join in and play a co leadership role of caring and respectfulness to each other to enjoy the future in jobs. We are seeing more reports and focus to our workplace issues in bullying, aggression, trauma, incidents, poor behaviour being more discussed, but with what result or outcome. The environment has to the be the first place of action, before we can begin to tackle the unfair behaviour, we actually do it upside down. We tackle the poor behaviour first as the first get out clause. By retraining the individual or team members who have caused the issues, or performance management them over a period of time, move them to another area of the business or look to put pressure so as the person will be forced to leave. But most approaches by companies will be to find the person or members responsible then work out strategies to manage then out. But the culture or the environment of the organisation is never considered, or companies and managers just hope it will all go away die a natural death, be all squared away, but guess what, it happens again, again and again.

The work that is being done at GP Bridge Training and Development is environment focus first, 'you have to know where you are in the workplace 'Now' and to know where you want to be in the future'. Then you can begin to work through the maze of the poor behaviours. Its no different in a toxic family environment that just bleeds fear, ego and control and then you see the secret lies and betrayals appear, then you're in real trouble. Businesses need to realise and be proactive to environmental care and planning. We can throw all the resources into implementing health and exercise programs in the business environment but if it is not well and unhealthy underneath your back to square one. We are seeing businesses adopt strategies to improve their workplace and looking to alternative approaches as they value their staff and how best to keep their staff and work out arrangements in their workload to come to a win-win outcome. As we move into the future, we will see a transformed way of work being operated like never before. I am not sure what shape it will look like, but I am sure it will be different to what we are seeing now and in the past.

Looking in reflection to the past and where we are all now, many personal experiences have been in bedded and locked in our memory. When our health, our workplace toxic environments and poor outcomes could've all been avoided by preventative and conscious attitudes behaviours. To think right now there are people in positions who are contemplating shifting to moving to another company or just leaving their professions to get away from the madness and chaotic display of behaviours that serves no one positively. Companies do feel the brunt and the loss of great people committed to make a difference. I am extremely positive and optimistic of the work companies and the workforce are looking to engage with each other to form new leaderships into the future. The opportunity for everyone to keep health in mind our personal health in check and monitor ourselves more regularly, take responsibility for our ongoing management of ourselves is paramount. We only have one life, we must nurture it, harness it, be conscious of it and enjoy being who we are with great fun and vitality. Let's hope in the future we can all prevent illnesses and reduce potential stresses that we have a great life along the way and encourage other to do also. As I mentioned earlier in this book, I wanted to bring some awareness and conscious thought to our personal position on our health. I have through my years have witnessed great and talented people who have had their professional lives cut short. With future generations on the way, we must look to build a foundation of great hope and encouragement, so they can enjoy the positive fruits of the work that has been done until now. To inspire our workplace community to getting up out of bed each day feeling better than they were yesterday is a good starting point. Let's all contribute to improving the workplace environment so we can all show our class and be proud of it and who knows what great opportunities come from that, it's worth working towards.

'What the sad fact about it is, is that we can prevent most of our illnesses and our workplace can be a possible high cause or influence on our chronic illnesses outcomes. In the end, for it to take my own life is something I did not sign up for'.

The Human Behaviour Excellence Centre

Our Team and Programs

At the Human Behaviour Excellence Centre, we form part of a group of committed businesses with Deadly Training and SAFCOM to inspire and provide enhancement of skills and knowledge for both businesses and individuals. We conduct varied and flexible delivery to meet the needs of the client without causing great disturbance to productivity.

Our programs have been delivered both in Perth and in regional Western Australia. It is our future focus to deliver to all parts of Australia. Our programs are all of self-awareness to improving workplace relationships, with an inclusive approach to bringing the workforce closer together.

GP Bridge Training and Development

Would you like a workplace culture that;

1. Improves on workplace disruption
2. Reduces absenteeism
3. Decreases aggression, bullying and other unacceptable behaviour

4. Reduces risks and costs for compensation claims, legal and litigation expenses

5. Expands positively on your reputation, profile and image

6. Advances personal health, business relationships that impacts on productivity, the work environment and your future life

If you are looking to achieve great rewards and empowering outcomes in your workplace culture, then you should attend our workshops to strengthen and enhance your business, your workplace personnel or your life in general.

What does GP Bridge Training and Development do?

Our focus is to positively enhance and inspire your workplace utilising practical teaching and education methods that provide confidence and a safe work environment.

We help your organisation in where you are *now* and where you would like to *go*.

We re-engage employers, employees and associates through awareness that restores and builds improved culture of health and behaviour environment that inclusively gets great outcomes.

In partnership with Deadly Training

Cultural Awareness Course

Conducts flexible delivery courses in Indigenous training to assist in the understanding of Aboriginal cultural diversity and to businesses. Indigenous training is an inclusive delivery program, with Indigenous facilitators who come from strong culturally and with experience. These sessions are conducted either half day days or full time to meet the client's needs and not disrupt the workplace.

So, if you are looking to attend a cultural awareness program, why not speak to our team.

A New Era in Business Direction

GP Bridge Training and Development also delivers its new course, 'A New Era in Business Direction', which is designed to educate and skill businesses and their employees to understanding the shift in our future workplace. The workplace is becoming an ever-changing environment for both business and employees. We have identified that there are key areas to future workplaces keeping their reputation, profile and goodwill in tact that will engage and enhance their branding going forward.

They cover areas such as;

A.   **Entrepreneurial World**

- The world has shifted and more people are establishing new businesses
- We have seen a huge increase in women entering the business field with small start ups

B. **Our Health status**

- Our increase in unhealthy business community has seen an increase in depression, stress, mental illness etc
- What is this doing to our workforce and where is it likely to move in the future?
- What long term costs are associated to high costs of illness in the workforce?
- What strategies can be implemented to addressing health issues?

C. **Engaging of women in the workforce**

- We are seeing an increase in women promoted into more senior positions
- More women are entering or re - entering the workforce
- A new way of behaviour or approach to engaging women in the workforce is required

- Being mindful that the increase of bullying and unfair behaviour to women in the workforce has increased

- What steps and approaches can be implemented to harmonise our workforce?

D. **Difference in hard skills and soft skills**

- Our connection in the workforce has been disconnected through technology

- What ways and approaches can we best look at to engage our workforce to reintroduce the soft skills?

- It's not all about the qualification. Our ability to provide a more effective solution driven approach, while building and establishing connection with our clients

E. **Drilling down in our destination**

- What is our business purpose?
- What direction are we going?
- What do we need to get there?
- What tools and resources are required to get there?
- What steps are required to get there?

F. **Cultural Diversity**

- We are seeing more cultural diversity in our business community
- The Indigenous community and the importance of it
- How best to spread the word on cultural awareness?
- How businesses need to integrate their workplace with more effective cultural awareness programs
- How our language use can either divide or bring our community together
- Open Space forum
- Q&A workshops

G. **Reputation**

- Our business reputation is on the line
- Our social media connection - is it impacting on our reputation?
- Are our communication styles effecting our reputation?
- What internal challenges are there in our reputation with the company structure?

- Strategies to repair your reputation in terms of issues the company faces in risks, financial and poor service to the community?

H. **Language use**

- Our language use in the workplace is more apparent than it's ever been
- The use of social media and how we convey our communications will have long term effects on our business and individuals
- The skilling of staff understanding language use and how it's communicated will leave us with an outcome in one form or another

I. **Generational Differences in the Workplace**

- We now have five generations in the workforce
- Each generation brings different values and purpose to the workforce
- How do we engage with each generation and communicate to work effectively?
- What strategies can be used to engage a more positive workforce?
- Industrial Age to the Conceptual Age

J. **Moral Leadership**

- Are companies being authentic and responsive to their staff and business ethics?

- Are our leaders showing the way with responsive leadership?

- Are we demonstrating 'inclusivity' in our workforce?

- Is what we are saying congruent to what we are doing? This brings not only clarity, but reduces inconsistencies which impact on business and internal relationships

K. **Ready for Beyond 2030**

- Are we doing business that will suit the future?

- How do we best communicate with our business partners?

- Will we need to be more collaborative with our local businesses?

- What is the best business approach to moving our business in the future?

- Is it our branding approach that will drive our business in the future?

- What challenges are there in moving forward?

- Are we challenged with the impact of robots, artificial intelligence, automation and can we implement these approaches for more productive business growth and long-term potential?

L. **Changes in the workforce**

- What future changes are there?
- Will staff be required to upskill themselves in a qualification, skill sets approach?
- Will technology of robots etc shift our business?

M. **Reinventing yourself**

- Are you doing your best work?
- What would happen today if you lost your position? Where would you go and what would you do?
- What personal resources would you be able to bring?
- What personal issues would impact on you moving forward?
- How would one cope in being made redundant?

- What are the exterior issues one faces to being laid off?
- What implications would there be to the family being made redundant?

N. **New work blend workplace**

- How can we manage people in our workplace for the future in share and time management with staff?
- Are we now looking for alternative ways to manage and coordinate staff in the workplace?
- Are we facing more work being performed in our homes instead of commuting to work?
- Are we progressing to more flexible work hours in working with our lifestyle?

O. **Pick yourself**

- What stops us moving forward?
- Is fear a driven force to impact on our growth as a person or business?
- Why is it that we wait to be chosen or be picked?

- Do we value ourselves enough to get our business and life going and be the champion we feel we are capable of being?

The opportunity for your business to expand its potential and move into the future, having a holistic approach and focus in your business and better engagement with your staff this program is most suitable to.

For more information on Deadly Training you can contact **Greg Bridge** at email gpbridge3@gmail.com

Business Beyond 2030 -What will your workplace look like?

In partnership with SAFCOM

SAFCOM director Greg Comans and Greg Bridge deliver their joint passion presentations to the business sector, on where the workplace will need to be Beyond 2030 with your Risk Management requirements and to the challenges of health and behaviour. All are most important to blending the business and Corporate World together moving into the future. We encourage you to book both Greg Comans and Greg Bridge and hear them give you an insight into the future of business that will minimise your costs and risks to your business. They also conduct in-house training to Risk Management and Health Behaviour Workplace practices that will enlighten and bring awareness to safe business practices.

For more information about Business Beyond 2030 you can contact Greg Comans on gcomans@safcom.net.au or Greg Bridge on gpbridge3@gmail.com

Visit our online shop: www.whitelightshop.com

www.ingramcontent.com/pod-product-compliance
Lightning Source LLC
Chambersburg PA
CBHW071906290426
44110CB00013B/1303